CLARE

with Peter O'Connell

www.**HERO**BOOKS.digital

HEROBOOKS

PUBLISHED BY HERO BOOKS
1 WOODVILLE GREEN
LUCAN
CO. DUBLIN
IRELAND

Hero Books is an imprint of Umbrella Publishing
First Published 2021
Copyright © Peter O'Connell 2021
All rights reserved

A CIP record for this book is available from the British Library

ISBN 9781910827376

Cover design and formatting: jessica@viitaladesign.com
Ebook formatting: www.ebooklaunch.com
Photographs: Inpho, Peter O'Connell, John Kelly (*The Clare Champion*) and Eugene McCafferty

★ DEDICATION ★

To my wife Lorraine
And to our daughters Eimear and Aisling.
I'm clearly outnumbered but I have to admit that the
three of you have great patience!

★ CONTENTS ★

★ ACKNOWLEDGEMENTS ★

IT HAS BEEN a privilege to create this book, particularly during a time when lockdown and Covid-19 were such dominant factors in our lives.

I'm especially thankful to everyone who agreed to be interviewed. What shone through, from the most experienced (Naoise Jordan) to the youngest (Tony Kelly) of the hurlers featured, was their unfailing love of the game and of their own place.

Whether they played in the 50s or are still wearing their club and county jerseys, the common link was their recognition that the game was handed down to them and their pride in wearing the jersey when it was their time.

Talking to these great men, I almost felt I was with them in the dressing-room, such was their depth of feeling when recalling times and games, sometimes from decades back.

I hope that I have lived up to the level of trust they put in me to carry their stories. A number of their tales and recollections are very personal and revealing.

Some of the chapters allow us to peer behind the curtain of inter-county hurling, where we see that the honour of playing for Clare can be as challenging as it is sometimes fulfilling.

Many people have been of invaluable help to me in writing this book, notably my wife Lorraine, whose experience as a sub-editor was never more appreciated!

I'm also very thankful to Liam Hayes of Hero Books for approaching me in the first place and then for editing 'Game Of My Life'. It was great to work with Liam and his team at Hero Books and to draw upon their advice and expertise.

My former *Clare Champion* colleague John Kelly was very generous in supplying a number of photos. I spent many days driving to and from Munster Championship matches with John, whose eye for a shot is incomparable.

You were assured of two things travelling to matches with John and Seamus Hayes; you'd be there hours before throw-in and you wouldn't go hungry. The main issue to be ironed out before departing was where and when were we stopping to eat. They were great days and all part of the experience of reporting on Clare teams.

Eugene McCafferty in Shannon also helped out on the photographic front and it's always a pleasure to work with Eugene. Michael O'Connor and Adrian McGrath loaned me GAA history books, which were exceptionally helpful. I'll have the books back to both of you well before Christmas 2022.

I also want to acknowledge the immense value of Seamus O'Reilly's book, 'Clare GAA – The Club Scene 1887 to 2010', and Pa Howard's collection '1949-2001' which is an invaluable history of Clare hurling teams at all levels. Both books gain in value and significance year-on-year.

The Clare County Library was a superb resource on the research front, as it houses a collection of all local newspapers, including *The Clare Champion* from 1903 to the present day. The library was an excellent source in my efforts to find details of some of the matches featured.

I hope that people in Clare, the diaspora and indeed GAA people across the country, find this book of interest. While of course the focus is on hurling, there are some slivers of insight into how Ireland has evolved as a society across the decades.

I have been involved with my local club Shannon Gaels GAA all of my life, on the playing, management and administrative fronts, along with Cúil Gaels LGFA.

Although I'm from West Clare, which is primarily a football-orientated part of the county, I can assure readers that the Clare hurlers are always supported to the hilt by the people of the west.

My first memory of a big hurling game was the 1986 Munster final in Killarney. In the excitement of Gerry McInerney's early goal, I lost my new crepe hat, which flew into the air and was never seen again. That day, I also lost every penny I had (£5) to a three-card-trick. So overall, it was a seminal few hours in Fitzgerald Stadium.

I later worked with Gerry for 18 years at *The Clare Champion* and I'm delighted that he is one of the 30 hurlers featured in this book.

On a final note, I would like to thank my parents Martin and Helen for fostering a love of sport in myself and my two brothers David and Damien.

Thanks again to everyone who helped me build this book.

Peter O'Connell
September 2021

NAOISE JORDAN

KILKENNY 6-10 CLARE 5-7
Wembley Tournament Final
Wembley Stadium, London
MAY 24, 1958

Naoise Jordan speaking at the unveiling of the Michael Cusack statue at Cusack Park in Ennis, and (inset) the front cover of the 1958 Wembley hurling programme.

★ **CLARE:** M Hayes; J Purcell, B Hoey, B Burke; B Dilger, D Sheedy, M Blake; M Lynch, N Deasy; J Smyth (1-4), M Nugent, M Dilger (0-1); P Kirby (0-2), G Ryan (2-0), **N Jordan**. Subs: J Rohan (1-0) for Lynch and C Madigan (1-0) for Deasy.

★ **KILKENNY:** O Walsh; T Walsh, J Walsh, J Maher; P Buggy, M Walsh, J McGovern; J Sutton (0-3), M Brophy; D Heaslip (1-0), M Kenny (0-2), J Murphy (0-3); S Clohessy (3-0), B Dwyer (1-1), M Fleming (1-1).

THE ACTION

THE CLARE HURLERS were given a unique and indeed history-making opportunity in May of 1958 to perform at Wembley Stadium in North London. They played 1957 All-Ireland champions Kilkenny in the first competitive hurling game played at the home of the English FA.

At the time, many thousands of emigrants from Clare, and throughout Ireland, had flocked to the English capital in search of employment and opportunity not as easily accessible in their own country. The presence of tens of thousands of Irish people in London and throughout Britain was central to the GAA's decision to rent Wembley Stadium.

As it transpired, the games in 1958 attracted a crowd of 33,240; an attendance which would have been higher were it not for a bus strike in London at the time. Clare qualified for the Wembley final following a 3-9 to 2-11 win over Waterford (a game that was played in Waterford on November 9, 1957).

As for the final against the Kilkenny men, there was an element of controversy over the awarding of one of the winners' goals. Seán Clohessy was credited with three goals but after the game, he acknowledged that his third goal had hit Clare goalkeeper Michael Hayes on the chest and deflected over the bar. However, the official scoreline stood at 6-10 to 5-7.

Amongst the Clare men to light up the lush Wembley sward were Ruan's Jimmy Smyth, who excelled in the second-half, while Dermot Sheedy, a very young Naoise Jordan and Johnny Purcell also played very well.

Hurling was described as 'Hockey with the lid off' by the *Daily Telegraph* GAA correspondent for the day.

★ ★ ★ ★ ★

66

THE TOURNAMENT WAS called The Monaghan Cup and in 1958 the GAA decided to play it in London. Kilkenny and Waterford had played in the All-Ireland final in 1957. What the GAA were anticipating was that they would have a repeat of the All-Ireland at Wembley.

We went down to Waterford to play them in the semi-final. Tom Cheasty was in his prime at the time, but Waterford let him off to play with their junior football team.

At half-time, we were eight or nine points up. They got worried. So one of their officials left the hurling match, and went and stopped the football match. They brought Cheasty back and, Jesus, with three minutes to go… they had drawn level. He came on for the last half an hour and he changed the game.

We got a free in! Jimmy Smyth was our normal free-taker. But Jimmy said to Pat Kirby, the famous handballer… 'Pat, throw that over the bar!'… which he did and we won by a point.

Going in at half-time, Johnny Purcell and Tolly Guinnane were saying, 'Keep it up lads… we're in Holyhead already!' By the time the match was finished, our Holyhead ticket was nearly gone. Funny enough, we ended up flying from Shannon.

We were on our way to Wembley.

Vincy Murphy, Dermot Sheedy and Noel Deasy were working in Shannon Airport at the time. Vincy, who was the Clare County Board delegate to the Munster Council, was organising us at the airport and the boys were laughing. Vincy was giving out like hell that Dermot and Noel knew the run of the place but still they weren't giving him any help.

When we got to London, we checked into the hotel and they decided that we'd go down around Piccadilly Circus. Vincy was in charge, of course. We'd be waiting to get on the Tube and Vincy would count us.

When we got off, he'd count us again.

We went to London on the Saturday and we were back on the Monday. It was the first hurling match played at Wembley. It was a huge thing back home and for the Irish community in London. There were over 33,000 at the match that day.

There was a bus strike in London at the time and they made out, only for that, there would have been a bigger crowd.

The surface was like a carpet. Mick Hayes and Ollie Walsh were the two goalkeepers and they had fair puck-outs. A few times they drove their puck-outs wide because the pitch was that bit shorter than a GAA one. But no matter what surface you're on, the goals are the same width. If you can't put it between the posts in your own field, you won't do it in Thurles, Croke Park… or Wembley.

While it was a great occasion, I felt I hadn't a great game. I was only 18 and I really didn't get the kick out of it that I should have got.

I think Michael 'Gruggy' Dilger from Ennis was the first man to score a point at Wembley.

The craic we had in the hotel was great. I wasn't drinking and it wasn't a boozing session but it was great fun. We met an amount of Clare people. After the match, I met a friend of mine from Whitegate, Joe Collins. I gave Joe my hurley.

He came back home from England after a good few years. He was living in Whitegate and didn't his brother John take the hurley out and break it. He went and got it repaired, and it's hanging up now in the clubhouse in Whitegate.

I was on the Clare minor team in 1956 but Cork destroyed us below in Mallow. I was eligible again in '57 but I went working for McInerney's in Cork at the time. The procedure that time was that you had to fill up your application form, including things like your date of birth. The Clare County Board missed out on that, with the result that I wasn't on the minor team in 1957.

A month later, I was on the senior team. We played Kilkenny in the Oireachtas. I didn't make the minor team but I made the senior team.

When I think of that day below in Kilkenny… I was in the same dressing-room as the likes of Mick Hayes, Matt Nugent and Johnny Purcell. My brother Paddy was also on the panel. I was looking around in awe at those fellas.

Paddy and myself went together by car from Cork. A card had been posted to the digs. I remember the morning I got it. We were in separate digs and when I was going to work with Paddy that morning, I said that I was after getting a card from Michael McTigue [Clare GAA secretary] to play for Clare the following Sunday week.

Paddy said to forget about it, that I had plenty of time to play for Clare. I was six feet off the ground when I got the card. Next thing, I was on the ground. Two days after, we were going up to work again and wasn't Paddy after getting a card as well. Everything was alright then.

He was full-forward and I was wing-forward.

That was his last game for Clare and it was my first. There were 12 of us in the family and Paddy was second from the top. He won a Railway Cup with Connacht in 1947. He was a good hurler. He did most of his hurling in Ballinasloe because he was working there.

Dan McInerney had finished up hurling in 1956 but twice a week I had to bring my hurley and boots to work. Dan would arrive on the job at 3pm twice a week. He'd pick me up and we'd go out to Kilbarry, which is a park about a mile outside Cork. We'd hurl there for two hours and he'd have me back on the building site for the lift home.

Pádraig McMhatúna used always say to me that I was the first professional hurler. 'You got paid for hurling,' he used to say to me.

I was in Cork for about eight months and I went from there to Croke Park. They were building the Hogan Stand at the time. That one has since been demolished and the new one built.

One of the other Clare games I remember well is the 1967 Munster semi-final. I thought I had a good game that day. It was in Limerick and there was a big crowd at it. We had beaten Limerick in the first round but Tipperary beat us well in the Munster final.

Training was fairly limited. We'd meet at St Flannan's College. John Hanly was our coach and Colum Flynn looked after the physical side of things. We'd do a couple of rounds of the field, a bit of leap-frogging, a bit of hand-passing... then we'd have backs and forwards.

That was it.

There was no gyms and no problems with hamstrings. We never heard of them.

I was working in the buildings and anywhere you went that time, you either walked or cycled. I went to the vocational school in Scariff and that was nine miles from Whitegate. I'd cycle morning and evening, five days a week. You're talking nearly 100 miles a week... *how could I pull a hamstring?*

We won nothing but we got great enjoyment out of it. Seán Cleary, Eamon Russell, Noel Casey, Tony Marsh, Jackie O'Gorman and myself were in our own group. The Newmarket crowd would be together, and the Clarecastle crowd would be together. We got great enjoyment out of it.

I last played Munster Championship for Clare in 1969 and I played in the Intermediate Championship in '71. That was the end of the story.

One of the club games I remember well is one of the first I played for Whitegate. It was about 1955 or '56. I was 16. It was a double-header in Feakle for the Monsignor Hamilton Cup. It was to raise funds to develop pitches in the county.

Des Carroll was refereeing it. Scariff played the Mills in the first match and we played Feakle in the second game.

I got the ball about 30 yards out on the wing. I turned and hit it. There it was, sailing over the bar. And what happened? While the ball was still flying through the air, but not yet gone over the bar, didn't The Angelus bell start ringing.

The church is near the field in Feakle.

What did Des do? He blew the whistle and we stood up and said The Angelus. Then he brought the ball out to the '21' and threw it in. I got no point but we still won the match.

Whitegate had won their first championship in 1950. Ned Doyle, my brother Paddy and Jim Kenneally were on the 1950 team. We also had a good team from 1957 up to the early 60s.

We won one in 1961 and got beaten in three other county finals. We also won the Clare Cup a couple of times. The year we won it, we beat Newmarket in the final... and that was the start of the great Newmarket team. The likes of Pat Danaher and Puddin' [Jimmy Cullinan] were 18 or 19 at the time. They were only starting.

We were lucky in a way. Ruan were champions in 1959 and '60. Newmarket beat them in the semi-final in 1961. I'm not so sure would we have beaten Ruan in that final. They came back in 1962 and won it again. John Duggan was in goals for Newmarket against Ruan in the 1961 semi-final. He made a save from Jimmy Smyth in the last couple of minutes, when Newmarket were two points ahead.

I always associated that with the Art Foley save from Christy Ring. Every time I'd meet him, I'd say, 'I've a county championship medal, thank you!'

I'd never have been heard of but for Tom Cleary, who played centre-forward for Whitegate. I also had a great understanding with Michael Doyle.

When we were training for the 1961 county final, Fr Liam Murray was our coach. Caimin Lynch did the training and Tim Kelly was a selector. We were out on the field nearly every second evening, doing the hurling skills. I feel presently that hurling has gone a bit robotic.

There's nobody hurling from instinct now. Back then, that was all you had. Now, you're told to hit it to a spot and there's supposed to be a fella there waiting for it.

I never played any other sport aside from hurling.

There was nothing else to do. We'd often be in the hurling field three times on a Sunday. There used to be two Masses in Whitegate and after Second Mass, a few would accumulate outside the gate. Someone would say, 'We'll go for a few pucks!'

Our house and Doyle's house were either side of the hurling field. The hurleys would be left into the two houses. We'd hurl until dinner time.

After that, the hurling field was the place to be. The Mountshannon lads used to cycle down; Tom Turner, Ned Cahill, Tom Cleary and the lads.

We'd stay hurling until a few farmers' sons would have to go home to do the milking. That time, religion was a bit more prominent and there would be a rosary on the Sunday evening. When you'd come out after the rosary, it was down to the hurling field again.

It wasn't easy to get hurleys at the time. They were scarce enough.

The best hurley marker that I ever got a hurley from was James Conway from Larchhill in Ruan. He used to make a lovely hurley. It could play on its own. I can't remember breaking too many hurleys. Then again, I wouldn't have been a great mixer in that I hadn't the physique. I was light and I kept out of the way.

They used to say I was quick but I didn't think I was; I was a good reader of the game. I could read it well. You can look quick if you're in the right place at the right time.

I transferred from Whitegate to Parteen in 1977.

We won the Junior B league and championship that year. Wolfe Tones beat us in the junior A final in 1979. Look at what they have achieved since!

My favourite position was left wing-forward. My one regret in my hurling career was when I played corner-forward; I did what I was told and stayed inside on the end line. I should have been out around the '21'. I had no business standing beside John Doyle.

I should have thought about it more and took it on myself to go out. If the ball doesn't come to you, you should be going looking for it. And it wasn't coming that often.

The best players I played with were Jimmy Smyth, Puddin Cullinan and Matt Nugent, who was a great ground hurler. He was a pure gentleman of a hurler. Puddin was in a class of his own. For the size of him, he took on and beat the best of them. He was great craic as well. He was an entertainer. I used to love being in his company.

It might have been rough enough on the field but when it's over, it's over.

Once you played hurling for Clare, you're always remembered as a county man. At times, you get more credit than you deserve, especially as time goes on. But wherever you go, if you have played for Clare, you'll have friends and you'll have people who will come up and talk to you and ask you about matches.

They wouldn't criticise you if you lost.

There's no need for anybody to tell you or write that you're playing badly. It's like when you're going in at half-time... you know if you're playing well or badly.

You won't be waiting for a selector to tell you.

You'll know yourself.

99

JACKIE O'GORMAN

CLARE 2-9 WEXFORD 2-7
Oireachtas Cup Quarter-Final
Kennedy Park, New Ross
SEPTEMBER 17, 1967

Jackie O'Gorman enjoyed a winning afternoon against Wexford in his first appearance for the Clare seniors, but he also received a lesson or two from Phil Wilson that he never forgot.

★ **CLARE:** P O'Brien; M Considine, M Bradley, J Nevin; **J O'Gorman**, V Loftus, E Russell; L Danagher, T Ryan (0-2); N Pyne (0-2), M Arthur, P Cronin (0-4); P McNamara (1-1), J Cullinan, M Keane (1-0).

★ **WEXFORD:** P Nolan; T Cotton, E Kelly, E Colfer; V Staples, D Quigley, L Rigley; J Murphy, J Galway (0-1); P O'Donoghue (1-1), P Lynch (1-3), P Wilson (0-1); T O'Connor, S Whelan, J Quigley (0-1).

THE ACTION

NEW ROSS IN mid-September 1967 was unseasonably wet and overcast. The sunny South-East it definitely wasn't. For the hurlers of Clare and Wexford, the weather was not their primary concern.

Their sole aim was to qualify for the semi-final of the Oireachtas tournament, which at the time was still regarded as a prestigious competition.

Clare dominated the game and had they availed of the many chances they created, they would have won more comfortably.

In fact, Clare had enjoyed a reasonable 1967. The had reached the last four of the National Hurling League, losing to Kilkenny. Successive Munster Championship wins over Limerick and Galway had propelled them into a final meeting with Tipperary in Limerick. They fell to a double-digit defeat that day, losing 4-12 to 2-6.

Some of their issues in that Munster final defeat manifested themselves again in New Ross. Winning possession wasn't a problem but converting it into scores was - the fact that Wexford goalkeeper Pat Nolan was their busiest player in the opening half helps to illustrate how dominant Clare were. The scoreboard did not reflect that and, in fact, Wexford led 0-5 to 0-4 at half-time.

Narrowly adrift at half-time to a team who were crowned All-Ireland champions in 1968, Clare were eight behind six minutes into the second-half. It was then that they began to show what they were made of. In the middle of the field, Newmarket's Liam Danagher began to dominate, assisted by the hard-working Tom Ryan. A goal from Paddy McNamara was pivotal and from there on, Clare clawed their way back into it. As the game evolved, the Clare full-back line withstood immense bouts of pressure from Wexford and having steadied themselves after the concession of those early second-half goals, they managed to repel the Yellow Bellies.

Pat Cronin and Noel Pyne played great hurling in the second-half, as Clare chiselled out a two-point win. They qualified for an Oireachtas semi-final meeting with Tipperary in Cusack Park on October 1, emerging with a 4-8 to 3-5 victory. On October 15 in Croke Park, they took on Kilkenny in the final. A couple of late scores derailed Clare at GAA head-quarters. Kilkenny ran out 4-4 to 1-8 winners and were crowned Oireachtas champions for 1967.

★★★★★

66

WHEN I WENT out that day, who was I lining out on… only Phil Wilson. He would have been an All Star about five times in-a-row at that stage… if there had been All Stars.

That time, there weren't too many country clubs up to a huge standard but they had a lovely little stand in New Ross. It was a two-eye hay shed for all the world. It had a roof but no sides, no back, nothing. But it was of the time.

Anyway, I thought… *Here goes. I'll be well able for this fella!*

After a few minutes, Pat Nolan pucked out the ball down on top of myself and Phil. Again, I thought… *This is no problem.* I was used to it from intermediate club hurling in Clare. I'd nearly win every one of these type of puck-outs.

I shaped up to it anyway, in all my glory. I was putting up a hand, high enough I thought, when Phil put his hand up a good bit higher and caught it. Off he went.

He took five or six steps towards the hay shed and drove it straight over the black spot. The hay shed was full and it reverberated. I thought 'twas going to fall. I was nearly hoping it would fall on top of me after that. That's the one thing I remember in all my years playing.

In 10 seconds, I got about two years' experience.

It wasn't about the winning or losing of it, but it was the very first day I played for Clare. I had been on the panel for a couple of years. Clare had a fine team at the time. They had got to Munster finals in 1964 and '67 but had lost the two of them.

At that stage, they were inclined to break up a bit. Seán Cleary, the 'Puddin' (Jimmy Cullinan) and Eamon Russell were the half-back line, and Seán retired.

So after a long wait, I got the call at No 5. I was 24 at the time. Wexford had a fine team. They had been beaten in the Leinster final by Kilkenny and they went on to win the All-Ireland the following year (1968).

So I was drafted in anyway. I was an intermediate club hurler with Cratloe. We weren't as lucky as we are now to have the bunch we have. I hardly ever played on an inter-county hurler in club hurling. The Puddin, Liam Danaher and Paddy McNamara were all senior players.

The Oireachtas was a big competition at the time. The provincial finalists used to play off a semi-final and a final. That time, Tommy Small from Parteen was vice-chairman of the County Board and he always had an auld grá for me and eventually he got me on the team.

Mostly, it was senior club players that were on the panel that time but Fr Harry eventually revolutionised it. There was a load of junior and intermediate club players in Fr Harry's team. Colm Honan, Pat and Enda O'Connor, myself and Tom Crowe, God be good to him. Harry threw the net wide. I think there were nine or 10 lesser-grade fellas on the panel.

The next day I went out, I wasn't as cocky.

I was a lot more cautious and I respected everyone around me. That was the real moment that stood out for me. We had loads of wins and losses but you take those with a pinch of salt. They only last a day or two.

The Oireachtas was huge back then, and even bigger before that. If you went back to 1954, Wexford and Clare played. Clare won the replay and there was 45,000 at it. The Oireachtas medal was also the nicest of them all. I never won one but I saw them in the distance… like a lot of the other medals.

There was great camaraderie when you'd meet lads off the field. The likes of Tony Doran and Willie Murphy would ate you on the field but they were as sound men as you'd ever meet off it.

The rules were kind of different that time; it was war inside the line and forget about it after.

The next big showdown was in 1968, when we met Kilkenny in the league semi-final. It was a draw twice and they beat us the third time in Thurles. Tipp beat them in the final afterwards. That was as near as we came to glory in the 60s.

After 1968, a lot of those lads, like Pat Henchy and Jimmy Smyth, packed it in. There were a couple of lean years then until about 1972. Clare got to an under-21 Munster final in '72. Seamus Durack played in it and in '74, they got to another one. Boys like Enda and Pat O'Connor, Stack, Loughnane and Hehir were on that team. All of the household names. But they lost both finals; the first one to Tipp, and the second one to Waterford, when they were roaring hot favourites.

But Fr Harry (Bohan) came along then and he picked a bunch from those under-21 teams.

In 1972 we played Limerick in the Munster semi-final.

Limerick were after winning the league. They came up to Ennis and they were hot favourites. We bate them anyway as it happened and we got to the Munster final against Cork.

I'll never forget what happened… and it wasn't anything to do with hurling. I was at home and I had a bit of hay to tram. Tony Considine's father was with me. He was a great man and a bit of a wit. We were going well the same evening. I had a bit of a front-loader and we were tramming to bate the band.

Anyway, I said to him, 'Tom, we'll have to leave the rest of it there 'til tomorrow'.

'Where are you going?' he asked.

I said that I had to go training to Ennis for the Cork match on the Sunday week.

He said to me, 'If I were you now, little boy, I'd stay here and tram my hay because ye're going nowhere against Cork down in Thurles'.

As it happened, the following day it rained and it rained for a fortnight. I had to push the hay up on the ditch. Tom was true to his word. Cork bate us by about 18 points.

But life went on… no one died.

As for pre-match meals and that, you'd get a plate of sandwiches and you'd ate them all. You'd be starved. It would take you three hours to get to the likes of New Ross. There was no such thing as eating properly. If you got to a Munster final and if you were lucky, you'd get steak and chips after training.

We were loving it. You'd have a pint with it and there'd be no problem. But, to be fair, the whole thing has moved on. GAA, soccer and rugby have all moved on.

In elite sport now, it's all about 'the system'. Individual flair has to blend into the system. They have trackers now in their jersey to check their mileage. In our time, the tracker mortgage wasn't even invented… let alone any other tracker.

But it's all for the good. I love to see young fellas getting on and doing their thing. The only problem I have with it is that, as an elite sport, it's unintentionally depriving a lot of lads from playing inter-county hurling. What I mean by that is, if you take the block-layer, the carpenter, the farmer or the agricultural contractor, they have no chance of doing the training that the teacher, the guard, the civil servant or the student can do.

If a fella has 200 cows to milk of a Saturday morning, what chance has he of making training? They're being squeezed out of it. The group is getting smaller. That's the only regret I have about it. You could have a flakin' hurler in a country place and they just wouldn't be able to give it the time.

I think present-day hurlers are super, I have to say.

We wouldn't be let into the dressing-room now.

In our time, you marked your man and the less he scored, the better job you were doing if you were a back. At the other end, if a fella scored a few points and was playing corner-forward, he was doing a great job.

But now there's no such thing as marking a man... it's marking space. The 'middle third' has also been invented. That was never there. You had four fellas in the middle of the field and they hurled away. But I have no problem with it; the world has moved on and it's great to see it.

The last Cratloe man to play for Clare before me was Pa Quain. He was on the 1946 team that won the National League. I was the next generation. We only had a small little playing pool. There was nothing like the development in Cratloe that we have had over the last 10 years. But times were good. We only won two or three intermediates but they were as good as All-Irelands to us.

From about 1975 on, Cusack Park in Ennis was closed and we played all our matches in Tulla. It was a fortress. We played about 30 in-a-row and never got beaten against all of the top teams. There was a huge buzz.

We got to the league final and drew against Kilkenny in 1976. They went off to San Francisco on the All Stars trip. I'd say we got caught in the fog a bit. We thought they'd come back a bit under the weather but they bate the hell out of us in the replay.

But the following year, we were ready for them.

The Clare crowd that time, the Lord save us... there'd be 2,000 Clare supporters at a challenge match. When we won the league in 1977, it was the first time since '46 that Clare had won a national title. 'Twas as good as two All-Irelands to a Kerry man and, personally, it was a huge thing.

There were lads... Puddin, Danaher and Paddy Mc, who were winning county titles with their eyes closed for Newmarket. They didn't know anything about defeat. But for a fella like me, who was only winning an intermediate now and again, 'twas huge. The following year, we won the league again and then we had the Munster finals in 1977 and '78.

Life was good.

'Twasn't all winning… 'twas great. I wouldn't change a bit of it.

That time, if you were lucky enough to have them, you'd probably bring two hurleys to a match. The second one would be a bad one because if you broke it, you'd get a new one going home. So you'd start with the bad one and after three minutes, it would be broken and you were in business. You'd have a second one going home.

Tom Mac (McNamara) was a selector in the early years before Fr Harry. Tom would have a 10-10-20 manure bag with a load of hurleys inside in it. There was no such thing as personalising your hurley. You'd be told to hurl away 'with that yoke'. That was the way.

I wouldn't like to be playing now.

Sure you could do nothing else if you were. I used to work in Shannon and I'd be tippin' away with a bit of land. I remember going into training one day above in Ennis on a Saturday about 11 o'clock, which was most unusual. Justin McCarthy was coaching us at the time. We were training away and there was no sign of (Mick) Moroney.

The next thing, Moroney arrived about a quarter of an hour later. I said to him, 'Were you dodging the early work?' He said he was after putting in 4,000 square bales before he came to training and that he wasn't able to wag.

While we never won much, we were a bit like the Mayo footballers in the sense that the nation took us to heart.

I often said that when we came home to Ennis after winning the league in 1976, t'was like the time Daniel O'Connell came to Ennis, there was such a crowd around.

In later years, I said to someone that we were very like the Irish soccer team, the whole country was mad about us and we won nothing.

But we had great auld times.

99

SEAMUS DURACK

CLARE 3-11 ANTRIM 2-5
National Hurling League Round Three
Lougheil
DECEMBER 6, 1970

'It was a way of life. I don't know how I would have turned out if I hadn't hurling,' admits legendary goalkeeper Seamus Durack.

★ **CLARE: S Durack**; C Hanrahan, G Lohan, O O'Donnell; J O'Gorman (0-1), T Slattery (0-4), M Moroney; J Cullinan (0-1), N Casey; J McNamara (1-4), M Culligan, J O'Donnell (0-1); P O'Leary, M Kilmartin, D Fitzgerald (1-0). E Hamill (1-0 og)

THE ACTION

THE WIND WAS blowing hard in North Antrim when the Clare hurlers visited for a pre-Christmas tussle with the home county. Two weeks before their trip, Clare won but conceded four goals against a weakened Kerry team in Tulla; so they didn't head for the glens, on the first Sunday in December, brimming with cast-iron confidence.

They probably felt that they needed to put some scores on the board if they were to quell Antrim's early enthusiasm. That's exactly what happened. Sandwiched between early points from Tom Slattery and Jimmy McNamara was a Dermot Fitzgerald goal for Clare, who shot the visitors into a 1-2 to 0-0 lead.

Antrim got going shortly after that when Barney Campbell let rip, but his effort was repelled by Seamus Durack on his debut. Eddie Donnelly had better luck on the goal-scoring front when he banged home Antrim's first goal, after a Seán Burns free had hit the Clare crossbar and come back into play. When Seamus Richmond netted the home team's second goal, it looked as if Clare were in for a long afternoon.

Antrim led by two points at half-time, but as the second-half progressed, their energy levels dipped.

Clare's right half-back Jackie O'Gorman began to dominate and picked up a vast amount of loose ball. In front of him, Jimmy Cullinan and Noel Casey ruled midfield, while Jimmy McNamara put away a crucial goal for the winners. McNamara was also central to forcing the Antrim corner-back Eamon Hamill into conceding an unfortunate own goal. Clare eventually left Lougheil with two points on the board. They faced into a long journey home, albeit one which would have felt much more taxing had they not won. Interestingly, a future Clare coach, Cork's Justin McCarthy, was on the line for Antrim that day, lending his coaching expertise to the Saffrons.

★ ★ ★ ★ ★

66

THE BALL CAME in and the partisan crowd were roaring for blood.

There was about a minute to go and Antrim had us on the run. I stopped the ball on the goal-line and it got stuck in the mud. I felt that the ball had to be removed out of there fairly lively.

Pulling on it wouldn't be enough to get it out of the muck. You had to try and get the hurley under it and flick it out. So it was taking that little bit longer.

Two of the forwards had me lined up, ball and all. Just as they were about half a metre away from me, I flicked the ball out for a '70'. The two of them met me and the three of us ended piled up as far back into the net as you can go. A big cheer went up from the crowd in Loughgiel.

They thought that the ball was in there with us but I'd managed to flick it away. That was my introduction to the National League and Antrim hurling. There was a lot of us in the net but the ball wasn't.

It was an early December day in 1970. The game was very tight and the temperature always seemed to be two or three degrees lower in the North the few times we played up there.

Paschal O'Brien was the goalie for Clare at the time. I was brought onto the panel as an outfield player. I had never played in goals at that level, although I had once or twice for Feakle. When we arrived in Dundalk the night before the game, I was asked by Bobby Burke, the County Board chairman, had I my goalie's hurley?

I never had a goalie's hurley in my life and I never had any intention of playing in goals. He said they had nobody else to go in goals and that I had played a few matches for Feakle… 'So you're in goals tomorrow!' That was my introduction to goalkeeping for Clare. I always wanted to play in the forwards or midfield and I had played outfield for the Clare minors and under-21s.

That time, Michael McTigue, who was the county secretary, would send a card, which was a bit bigger than a business card, telling you that you had been selected to play for Clare. It would also tell you that you would be collected at an appointed time. As a young fella, living in Feakle, it was a real treat to be collected and brought by car.

Tommy Nihill was the taxi driver and you had the likes of Vincy Murphy, who was the Munster Council representative, in the car. The GAA dignitaries would sit in the front and the players in the back. Tommy drove us to Dundalk, and on to Antrim.

Marie McInerney, who was a granddaughter of Dan McInerney the builder, had a cutting from *The Irish Press* the following morning when we went to work. Pádraig Puirséal had written the report and the heading was… O'GORMAN SHINES IN THE MUD.

It was a very wet day above in North Antrim and Jackie O'Gorman had a great game the same day. We won by a couple of points and we went on to qualify for the latter stages of the league.

The following month then, when it came to Munster Championship, Paschal came back training but one evening he decided that he had enough of it. I never asked him or spoke to him about it. I was getting a lot more play at my end, at the practice session at St Flannan's and the next thing he was gone. He went away.

That was the end of Paschal O'Brien's career and the start of mine. I was about 20 that time. I was at the top goals, the Enzo's Chipper side as we called it, and I remember Paschal going in over the stile. He never made any fuss and neither did the selectors. The jersey became an imprint on my back from there on.

When people look back at Clare trying to make a breakthrough in the 70s, it was Mount Everest every time to try and beat the likes of Cork. If they didn't catch you… Tipp would or Waterford or Limerick. We had great individual players but it wasn't until we collectively got together in the mid-70s, mainly through the good work of Fr Harry, that we had a focus on preparation.

Johnny Walsh was from the Mills and he did the physical training. Prior to that, it was a few rounds of the field and short-cuts being taken at cones by most players. You played with no hope. We were so unprepared for success, that failure became the norm.

We'd be told, 'Ye had a good match… ye did great!'… but we were always second-best.

We always played well in the second-half of every match because we could come to terms with the pace of the hurling and we knew that these fellas weren't that good. But we were so ill-prepared for the first-half, that they had the game won at half-time.

The likes of Cork and Tipp would switch off and we'd have switched on and won the second-half on the scoreboard. It was too late, though.

One of my distinct memories was of a selector from Feakle called Dan Cunningham, who used to drive a Volkswagen. There could be anything from a banamh to a heifer calf to a bale of straw in the car and he'd arrive to collect me. One day, we were going into Limerick but we had to do a bit of a detour. We went to Killaloe and around the country to collect a few other lads. We arrived in Limerick anyway and we pulled into the Gaelic Grounds car park.

I got out of the back of the Volkswagen and I still had the straw on my clothes. I had the pair of boots, socks and a hurley too.

The next thing, the Cork team arrived in big black cars that looked like Mercedes. We were watching Martin Doherty and John Horgan getting out of the cars. They looked to be about 10 foot tall. Psychologically, we weren't on the same playing field at all. We were completely ill-prepared… we were in awe of them. They could have won three minor All-Irelands and four under-21s and here we were going out playing against those fellas.

That was Clare hurling at the time and it's no disrespect to anybody. Playing for Clare was just never important enough.

We had a great under-21 team, which was beaten by Tipperary in the 1972 Munster final. We were good enough to beat Tipp that evening. We just couldn't fall over the line and win it. You'd nearly choke trying to hold out… and the level of desperation trying to defend!
We weren't mentally prepared for it.

We reached three league finals from 1976 to '78. We were beaten in the 1975 semi-final by a point by Tipperary, and in '79 we lost the league semi-final to Tipp by a point or two. During that time Cusack Park was being revamped and a lot of our league matches were played in Tulla.

By God, the atmosphere in Tulla and the rows between players, supporters and everyone was phenomenal. Then there was the after-match atmosphere in John Minogue's in Tulla. It went on until two or three in the morning. At that time of the morning, you could be interviewed by any fella who had a couple of pints in. You'd be fair game.

A favourite one that I used to get was… a fella might be eyeing you for a while, but wouldn't talk to you in a month of Sundays if he had no drink taken.

He'd be still eyeing you and he'd come up eventually… and say, 'Well, ye won anyway!'

You had to answer these lads. They'd remember what you said to them!

The next thing, he'd say, 'I thought you should have come a bit earlier to that last one'.

We could have had maybe two forwards coming in against one of our backs. The back had to go, but we had an understanding that the goalkeeper would come then.

Jackie O'Gorman or Jim Power would say to me, 'When I go, you have to be coming… take man, ball and all together!'

I was only a light fella but I went for them anyway.

I'd be telling this to the fella in Minogue's at three o'clock in the morning… that if I came out too early, the other fella would stick it in the back of the net.

The fella I'd be talking to might say, 'Jesus… maybe you're right!'

And he'd go away as happy as Larry that he'd got an explanation. He'd probably tell lads on the building site or the mart that he questioned the goalie the night before about whether he should have come off the line a bit sooner or not.

I savoured those times in Tulla.

People would have to park nearly half-way to Scariff with cars on both sides of the road. We'd be walking in with them with the hurley and the pair of boots. It was wonderful and it was casual. It was great for people because at that time there wasn't much else happening in Ireland in the 70s. We were going through a difficult time economically and people were emigrating. A lot of good people left.

Games kept everyone entertained. Lads would be having their breakfast or tea and they'd be talking about Stack being a 'noble hurler'… or someone hit another fella a 'right root'.

Life was very simple, but people had something to look forward to.

On the way to Thurles, I used to be looking out the window of the bus, seeing people eating sandwiches and you'd nearly be hungry looking at them. They'd be showing you the sandwiches but you couldn't eat them. Simple times. There was a bit of drinking and driving alright. Fellas would have three or four pints before the match and God knows how many after.

I'm not advocating drink driving but they were simpler times. It was a great time.

The game that gave me most satisfaction as a Clare man was the 1977 league final win, after being hammered in the replay the year before. After coming through so many years of winning nothing since 1946, we were National League champions. We had finally made the breakthrough against the team of that particular era.

We were finally receiving a trophy on a fine day with Thurles packed.

We had served our apprenticeship and we'd had good preparation from Fr Harry (Bohan), Colum Flynn, Jim Woods, Noel O'Driscoll, Gerry Browne and Justin McCarthy. In those years, we had good organisation and they embedded in our minds that we were as good, if not better, than these other counties.

Cork seemed to grow in stature when they played in the Munster Championship. They just had that belief. They were up four points before the match started at all. We got our chances to do it but we just couldn't. On the other side of this, we'd never have had the euphoria of 1995 and '97 if we had made those breakthroughs.

If there was a backdoor at that time, we'd have contested three or four All-Ireland finals for certain. No problem. We were caught on the day and we were caught by the *one* team.

I don't look back with regrets. I feel very fortunate to have been given the ability to play and the friends that I made out of it. I was never sent off for a foul stroke or anything like that.

The big thing locally was the county championship. Feakle weren't good at that stage but there was desperate rivalry going on between Newmarket, Clarecastle and Crusheen. There was no Sixmilebridge that time… they were very average. To the people of those parishes, to win the county championship was the All-Ireland final.

Inter-county was irrelevant, except for the actual players who played for the county. The skelping that was going on between Clarecastle and Newmarket… and several of the Clare panel from those two parishes! So they'd be on opposite sides of the dressing-room because they'd cut rashers off one another.

Then, you'd have a sprinkling from a few other parishes, and that was the make-up of the team.

I played handball with the Kirbys in Tuamgraney. I was playing against and watching the best handballers in the country at the time. They were phenomenal.

We used to play in the wintertime in the ball alley in Tuamgraney. We also had a good badminton team in Scariff and I used to play that, and we had a fair level of success. I also played a bit of rugby, while the ban was still in place. I enjoyed it, albeit at a fairly low level with Ballina-Killaloe or Scariff-Ballina-Killaloe. We had a mixture of teams at the time.

I played a cross-section of sport but I never left the hurley out of my hand.

In goal, if you have two good sides and you're sharp, quick and light on your feet, that helps. I was talking to Seamus Shinners, who played in goals for Tipp and Galway. He said that he spoke to a man about goalkeepers. This man said to him that what makes a good goalkeeper is not the hands, but the feet. *How quickly you can get down and move across the goals... side-step... get out... and move left or right.*

I'd communicate with the full-back line and tell them that all I wanted from them was two seconds.

One second to catch the ball, they check the man coming through... and two for me to clear it. I'd tell them not to worry about letting the ball into me, it was just that I didn't want man and ball at the same time.

I'd tell them that I'd take the ball as long as they body-blocked the man.

We were coming to the end of the 'man, ball and all' era but you were still going to get a bit of it. If you had a fella that was any way iffy, there'd be a bit left on you. It's hard enough to stop the ball, without getting the full-forward at the same time or just after. I'd have been known to verbalise that to my full-back line.

One of them would often say to me, 'Duke, you're blaming everyone else outside you bar yourself!'

I'd say, 'Sure, the ball had to pass all of ye before it came to me'.

We used to have a laugh about it.

It was a way of life. I don't know how I would have turned out if I hadn't hurling.

99

SEÁN HEHIR

As an 18-year-old student, a trip to Belfast for a hurling game led to an experience with the British Army that has lived with Seán Hehir.

66

THE RIFLES WEREN'T pointed up at the roof, they were pointed at our faces.

It was November 1971, and I had just been appointed captain of the hurling team at St Patrick's Teacher Training College in Drumcondra, in Dublin.

I was about to grow up very quickly. I went from being a young lad to realising that this world is not all about petty squabbles.

We were fixed to play Queen's University in a match up in Belfast.

I got my team organised and we got on the bus at about 8am that November morning. We had an arrangement made with Queen's that we were going to play the match on the Malone Road, overlooking Belfast. So we set off, full of the joys of spring. Everything was normal or so we thought. Then we got to the border. On the road up to Belfast, the border crossing was a different world. The bus was stopped and the driver was asked for identification, but he didn't have any papers.

The place was swarming with soldiers. The bus was in the middle of the road, so it was wheeled in to a place where there had been a cutting done in a hill. There was a wall of clay behind it.

The bus was boarded by fully armed soldiers.

It was very, very intimidating. They took possession of the bus like they were taking possession of an enemy street. We were ordered to stay sitting. Two of them went to the back with their rifles ready. You had two soldiers in the middle and two at the front... with the sergeant issuing the orders at the door.

I wasn't ready for this.

The question was asked... 'Who's in charge?'

At that stage, I didn't realise that I was the person in charge.

The next thing, it became obvious that I was, because there was nobody else on the bus to take charge.

I was 18 and the soldiers weren't any older than we were. They were just fresh-faced young fellas. I explained that we were going up to Belfast to play a match but they said that they had heard nothing about this. The next thing, the radio contacts were flying all over the place.

The message, from what was a Scottish regiment, was that they 'had a group here that were saying they are going to play a match in Belfast'. But we weren't to be allowed through.

The next thing we were ordered off... so off it we went.

The luggage compartment was then opened up and we were ordered to stand in a line, with our backs to the earthen wall behind us. The wall seemed miles high and we were surrounded by army people. We weren't going to be able to run from it.

I don't know how we survived it at all. I think it was my innocence that saved me. If you don't see the danger, it can actually save you.

The next thing, the soldiers asked that the person in charge get their bag from the luggage compartment.

I went up to get my bag and I also got my two hurleys.

'Hold it there. What's this?' I was asked.

I said that we were due to play a match in Belfast. He caught one of my hurleys and held it. I explained to him that this was what we use to play a match. Then somebody told him to let me go and I went back down to stand first in the queue.

Everyone else then got their stuff in turn. I had to go back up then and get the team gear.

What do you think happened then?

There was a bag left on the bus. It wasn't mine and it wasn't belonging to any of the players. Nobody volunteered that it was their bag.

'You're in charge!' I was told.

'Go up, carefully get the bag… open it… and stand back.' I got the bag and did as I was told. I stood back and they went through it… it was okay.

I'll never forget the loneliness of the walk for that last bag. It had nothing to do with me and I didn't know what was in it. As it turned out, I think it was a bag left from a previous run.

We were now standing on the side of the road, with what we thought looked like a firing squad ready in front of us.

This happened over 50 years ago and I still can't get it out of my head. Eventually, they got word back from Belfast saying there were apologies all round. Queen's University hadn't cleared it with the army that we were travelling to Belfast for a match. So we were allowed through.

We got back on the bus and headed up.

We played the match and we were absolutely useless. As the game was going on we heard the explosions going off down in the city. I'd say there were three explosions in each half, as the match was going on.

We togged in and Queen's gave us a bite to eat.

We got back on the bus and began the journey towards home. I was annoyed because we had done badly in the match and I was facing into a long year as team captain.

Malone Road is up over the city and that time, you came down through the city, before getting onto the motorway. Where did we have to go only right down, through the middle of the city, where all the racket was.

The next thing, some of the fellas at the back of the bus, who weren't playing but who had come up with us, started to throw shapes towards the loyalists and the army.

One of the lads came up to me and told me that this was going on down the back. He said that the next thing we'll have a rock through the window and we'll be in the middle of the riot.

I had to go back and explain to these fellas, who were my colleagues in college, that this wasn't on! I gave them an option. I asked the bus driver to stop and I told them that anybody who wanted to join the riot outside, that we'd open the door and let them out.

I said to them that the rest of us wanted to get home as safely as we could and that's what I intended happening.

We opened the door and nobody went out.

We closed it again and we crawled through what was mayhem between the loyalists, nationalists and the British Army thrown into the middle of it.

We eventually got out of Belfast and we made our way through the border checkpoint. God, was I relieved when we got down home.

Ger Loughnane was on that bus.

He was there in my year as well. He has never spoken about it, but he didn't have the stark experience that I had. PJ Fitzpatrick and Declan Kelleher were also on it, as far as I remember.

I could have told a different story altogether but that one haunts me. It's also of its time.

The following week, the college dean, who was a Fr Clyne, came to me and said, 'I hear you had a rather interesting outing to Belfast'.

I looked at him and said, 'I wouldn't want another one'.

After that, matches weren't played in Northern Ireland at all. They were played in a neutral venue around Dundalk. It was only afterwards, when I read about the Miami Showdown, that I thought… *At a flick of a switch, that could have been us.*

I can still feel the tension. As I'm talking about it now, *I'm cold.*

The sense of danger with young fellas, who were the same age as ourselves, with their rifles primed, standing right next to us.

Anything that came after that, in my hurling career, was a doddle.

I always regarded it as a close shave, a close shave that I walked into unprepared. The responsibility I had was crazy. We had about 40 young fellas on the bus, about to enter the prime of their lives.

It was the innocence of it.

We just walked into it.

COLM HONAN

CLARE 1-8 TIPPERARY 1-7
Munster SHC Semi-Final
Gaelic Grounds, Limerick
JULY 7, 1974

Colm Honan's first strike against Tipperary in the Munster Championship in 1974 was the first free he ever took as a senior player.

★ **CLARE:** S Durack; S Stack, V Loftus, J Power; G Loughnane, S Hehir, J O'Gorman; C Woods, M Moroney (O-1); N Casey (O-1), E O'Connor, **C Honan (O-6)**; J Callinan, G Lohan (1-O), M O'Connor. Subs: J Treacy for M O'Connor, J Cullinan for C Woods.

★ **TIPPERARY:** S Shinnors; L King, L Hackett, J Kelly; T O'Connor, M Roche, N O'Dwyer (O-1); S Hogan, PJ Ryan: F Loughnane (1-4), J Flanagan (O-1), P Byrne (O-1); J Keogh, R Ryan, M Keating.

THE ACTION

IN WHAT WAS a tough, rugged hour's hurling, Clare emerged from Limerick with a one-point victory and a place in the 1974 Munster final.

As evidenced by the final score, this game was neither free-flowing nor open. Both defences largely succeeded in keeping their attacking opponents fairly quiet. In this respect, the Clare half-back line of Ger Loughnane, Seán Hehir and Jackie O'Gorman were particularly effective, while Vincent Loftus was equally solid at full-back in front of Seamus Durack.

A first-half goal from Gus Lohan helped Clare into a two-point lead and it was an advantage that they protected manfully.

Tipperary were largely dependant on Francis Loughnane in attack, and he put away their goal about 10 minutes from full-time. It turned out to be Tipperary's last score and, while they piled on the pressure in their search for an equaliser, Loughnane missed a couple of scoreable frees.

At the opposite end, Colm Honan, on his debut, fired over six points, taking on the free-taking role for his county.

Seamus Durack made an exceptional save five minutes from time to maintain Clare's lead as Tipp pressed hard. Tipperary goalkeeper Seamus Shinnors made an equally impressive stop from Noel Casey. He managed to divert the shot around his post for a '70'.

Six of Clare's starting 15 - Seán Stack, Ger Loughnane, Seán Hehir, John Callinan, Colm Honan and Enda O'Connor - played in the Munster under-21 final a week later in Thurles. On that occasion, Clare were beaten 2-5 to 1-3 by Waterford.

In the years ahead, all played central roles in helping Clare to win two league titles in 1977 and '78 and in reaching successive Munster finals.

Two weeks after their semi-final win over Tipperary, Clare met reigning All-Ireland champions Limerick in the 1974 Munster final. Limerick won that game very convincingly, 6-14 to 3-9.

★★★★★

66

THE REASON I remember this game so well is because it was on a Sunday at 3.30pm... and the World Cup final was on at 5pm.

Holland were playing Germany, and my hero Johan Cruyff was playing for Holland. I was looking forward to the game because I loved watching him play. Himself, Mike Gibson and Muhammad Ali were my three favourite sportspeople at the time. As well as being supreme athletes, these guys were always in total control when performing.

Looking forward to that match put me in a relaxed frame of mind about making my debut for Clare, which served me well.

Tipperary had won the All-Ireland in 1971, but they were an aging team. Limerick had managed to beat them in the Munster final in '73, and our young team had beaten Tipperary numerous times as minors and under-21s. As a result of this we went into the game confident and at ease.

I was 20 years old and named at wing-forward.

With one of my first possessions I decided to take on Tadhg O'Connor on the outside. He took me down to concede a free, so I dropped the ball... and jogged on. This led to an awkward moment where I gradually realised that we didn't have a designated free-taker... a moment that ended when John Callinan roared... 'TAKE IT YOURSELF... FOR F**K SAKE!'

So I went back, took the free... and scored it.

And that was the beginning of my career as the Clare free-taker, a role I held for the next 10 years. It was my first time taking a free as a senior, because Dan Teefy was our free-taker for Clonlara and remained in the role for quite a while afterwards. As Clare's official free-taker, I started to practice. Back then if you scored a '70', it was considered magical.

If you missed one now for your club, you'd be dropped as free-taker.

Fr Harry (Bohan) was just in as manager at that stage and he had a big interest in hurling and was massively pro-player, the first time we had a supportive and sympathetic voice in management. He went on to put structure and organisation into the management of the team, bringing in proper coaching, strength and conditioning and a focus on skill development.

Later in the game I won a ball in the middle of the field and spotted Enda O'Connor open. He made a run and I put it into his hand. He burst through and set up our only goal. This became central to Seamus Hayes's account of the match in *The Clare Champion*. Seamus exclaimed at the tactical nous of someone passing the ball in hurling.

Even though we were at the top of the game and our skills were way ahead of previous decades, tactically, hurling hadn't moved on.

In the 70s I was a young Physical Education teacher in St Patrick's Comprehensive in Shannon Town. As well as helping the students develop their sporting skills, I promoted a healthy lifestyle, including being strongly anti-smoking.

I got a call from a Croke Park official one Monday to tell me that I had been selected for an 1978 All Star award, and he shared details of the awards ceremony in Dublin the following Friday. At the time, Carroll's cigarettes sponsored the hurling and football All Stars, and benefited from massive promotion, including the annual All Stars posters that were hung prominently in every local pub.

While I was thrilled and thankful to be selected as an All Star, I told him that I wasn't comfortable accepting an award that promoted tobacco. I knew that the iconic posters had already been printed, so Croke Park and Carroll's now had a problem on their hands.

I will resist the temptation to say a 'Major' problem!

This opened up frantic communication between the County Board, Croke Park and myself, as they tried cajoling, guilting and appealing to the prestige of the award to get me to accept it.

While there was considerable pressure on me to change my mind, I had put quite a bit of thought into the matter.

I stuck to my guns.

On the Wednesday, I got a final call from Croke Park asking what it would take for me to accept the award? I asked them to drop Carroll's as a sponsor. The GAA made a public announcement to this effect on the nine o'clock news that night.

The Taoiseach Jack Lynch hosted the banquet that Friday night, without a mention being made of the controversy. I was disappointed, but not surprised, to learn that Carroll's pulled the American tour planned for the following spring.

Despite this, I got great satisfaction from the incident.

We had repeatedly tried to push for greater player representation but had been shut down by County Boards and Croke Park, so it was good to get one small victory.

My first time playing a formal game of hurling was in St Flannan's, where I played alongside future inter-county stars but never won a Harty Cup. In my fourth year (1970) we had a great team, with Joe McKenna as captain, but we were beaten by North Mon in the Harty semi-final. The following year we lost the Harty final to Farranferris.

After the Leaving Cert, I got a scholarship to study PE at Strawberry Hill in London for two years, from 1971 to '73. It was a fantastic time for me because I got to spend it with some elite athletes. One student we used to watch training was David Bedford, who held the 10,000m world record.

John Phelan was an international athlete and knew Bedford. John asked him if we could train with him and run some laps. His training schedule, which we had never seen before, was interval running. He'd run 400m in 60 seconds… then he'd stop, take off his tracksuit top and fold it carefully. That was his interval before he ran another.

Then he'd get his tracksuit top back on and go again… doing 40 of those back-to-back. Myself, Jimmy Deenihan and Rory Kinsella kept up with him for the first five of them and almost collapsed.

Our hurling connection in these years came from London GAA clubs recruiting us from the college. One club, South and O'Hanlon's, would pick me up and bring me to their matches and the deal was that on the way home they would buy me a steak dinner.

We won a championship, but the hurling was very rough.

I remember in the London semi-final, I looked up to see Enda O'Connor lining up against me. I asked him, 'Enda, what are you doing here?'

'I might ask you the same inappropriate question,' he replied.

I loved London. Myself and Máire have four boys and three of them are now in London. Darach, the youngest, is the only one back in Clonlara.

In 1969, when I first started, Clonlara was a junior B club that hadn't won an adult title since 1951. By 1975 we had managed to win intermediate and get promoted, but the following year a number of the lads wouldn't even turn up for the fixtures. They'd say that we never did well in senior and we'd get relegated. That used to drive me mad.

In 1978, Clonlara had a cracking intermediate team and got to the final. Both Tom Crowe and myself were county players, with back-up from the likes of Fra Moloney, John Moloney and Dan Teefy. Unfortunately, Clare had recently lost the Munster final to Cork and I was cut up from the defeat and a long way from the carefree performance of my 20-year-old self. Clonlara went through the whole match against Ruan without scoring once. It showed the importance of psychology in hurling, another aspect of the game that has come on a great deal since my time.

I played my last game for Clare in 1985 against Tipperary. I spent 10 or 11 years playing senior hurling for Clare and it was the first time, in all those years, that Tipp beat us. I knew it was time to step back from inter-county after that.

I stuck my No 15 jersey in my bag and I must have received five letters from Robert Frost, the County Board chairman, looking for it back.

I kept it… and I still have it.

99

SEÁN STACK

SIXMILEBRIDGE 1-10 ÉIRE ÓG 1-7
Clare SHC Final Replay
Cusack Park
OCTOBER 31, 1983

The happiest half an hour of Seán Stack's hurling life was spent sipping a pint on the wall outside Peter Considine's after Sixmilebridge had won the 1983 county title.

★ **SIXMILEBRIDGE:** P Collins; J Keogh, N O'Gorman, K O'Shea; M Corry (0-1), J Brennan, **S Stack (0-1)**; F Quilligan, T Morey; J O'Connell, PJ Fitzpatrick, J Lynch (1-1); P Chaplin (0-1), D Chaplin (0-1), G McInerney (0-5). Subs: P Morey for M Corry, G Corry for P Chaplin, G Meehan for PJ Fitzpatrick.

★ **ÉIRE ÓG:** S Durack; P McMahon, P Kelly, J Barry; D Coote, M Glynn, F Heaslip; T Nugent (0-1), C Mahon; M Nugent (1-2), S Heaslip (0-3), S Lynch; P Lynch, P Barry, N Ryan (0-1). Sub: F Mahon for S Lynch.

THE ACTION

IT WOULD HAVE taken a thrilling county final replay to better the build-up to this game. In the drawn match, which was played on October 2, four players were sent off.

However, all four, Paddy Kelly and Paschal Mahon (Éire Óg), and Danny Chaplin and Pat Chaplin (Sixmilebridge), were free to play in the replay.

It was a replay that nearly didn't happen. Two Sixmilebridge players were on honeymoon, while others had holidays booked. The 'Bridge were not keen to play again until November 6.

The original replay date had been October 23. Éire Óg were awarded the championship by the County Board but the club executive refused to accept it. The clubs and County Board met and eventually it was agreed to hold the replay on Bank Holiday Monday, October 31.

As it turned out, the game was very sporting and there were no signs of any residual issues from the drawn encounter or indeed from the previous year, when the same teams also met twice in the county final. Éire Óg won the replay on that occasion.

Sixmilebridge led 1-7 to 1-4 at half-time in the 1983 replay, their goal coming from John Lynch, who fired beyond Seamus Durack. At one point they were 1-6 to 0-2 ahead and it looked as if they were going to win it easily.

Éire Óg rallied and Martin Nugent found the net for the Ennis men, while the same player also put over two points.

The second-half yielded just six points, evenly divided, while Éire Óg's John Lynch was the only man to land a score from open play during that period of play.

Sixmilebridge captain Gerry McInerney was presented with the Canon Hamilton Cup, the club's third senior championship. Full-back Noel O'Gorman received the Man of the Match award.

★★★★★

"

A GAME AND an occasion that stood out hugely for us was the 1983 county final. Éire Óg had a really good team, with players like Tony Nugent, Martin and Seán Heaslip, and Noel Ryan.

Michael Ryan was a very awkward centre-forward. He was a brother of Noel's. I got a bus out of Dublin after the All-Ireland in 1997; I missed my lift home and finished up getting a bus the following morning. *Who was organising the bus but Michael.* We had a great chat.

He told me that he got a job to do on me in the county final.

His job was to make sure that I didn't hit any ball… and he made my life a misery that day. If I went home to put the kettle on, he'd be there holding the kettle. He was in front of me everywhere I went.

He did a good job, I have to say.

Ourselves and Éire Óg drew the county final in 1982. In the replay, we went about 10 points ahead and lost. But the lead-up to the replay was a sad occasion the night before in Sixmilebridge. A good young fella, who was always pucking balls with us, got killed on the road that night.

We came across the accident coming home from a players' meeting. His father was our hurley maintenance man, a lovely, lovely man. He was always there for us.

What happened was very close to a lot of our hearts. I remember leaving his house at nearly 4 in the morning. His son was laid out in the county hospital in Ennis… word had come that he had died.

That took a huge toll on us. I think it hit us all at half-time in that match. We were well ahead but we lost that replay. That was a terribly low evening.

In 1983, we again met Éire Óg in the final.

Lo and behold, wasn't it a draw again. We won the replay and I remember for the hour after that match, everyone rushed up to Peter Considine's. I asked Tom Crowe, a great friend of mine, to go in for a pint of Guinness and to bring it out. The two of us sat on the bridge in front of the post office and drank our pints.

That was the happiest half hour of my life.

I hadn't smoked a fag in about six weeks. I bought 10 Major on the way up and it was the grandest half hour I ever spent.

It was the relief after the very sad events of the year before. Éire Óg were a good team and to come back and win it in a replay in 1983 would have been a highlight for me. Winning a Munster club in Centenary Year in 1984 was marvellous as well.

My last championship was in 1993, when we beat O'Callaghan's Mills. Then my wife convinced me that enough was *enough* and Sixmilebridge went out and won the All-Ireland a couple of years later. That'll tell you, I must have been more of a hindrance than a help!

I played my first senior game when I was 17 against Clarecastle.

The culture at that time was totally different. I think they bred these centre-forwards somewhere in the northern regions of Norway because they just came with a different agenda. Everybody knows the centre-forwards that played for Clarecastle, Newmarket and Brian Boru's!

They were more interested in destruction rather than construction. But that changed later on. I came up against the likes of Michael Ryan, who was awkward to play on but he wasn't out to break every bone in your body. Whereas, in the early to mid -70s, every centre-forward was designed to nearly kill you and that was his claim to fame. It changed eventually.

The 80s were marvellous times and we had some great games.

From my time with Clare, it's the defeats that stick with me. I often meet some of the players from back in the day. They remember the good days... and I say that it's the bad days that always haunt me.

You have regrets and you think about what if you had prepared better, or if the mentors had done this or that. Those are the questions that haunt every player, I think.

If you have a good day, cherish it because that fleeting moment only lasts a short time. When I hear players nowadays speaking about winning All-Irelands, leagues or county finals, they cherish the dressing-room immediately after the match, which is the vital part.

I had some great days but we never took time to ourselves to cherish the moment. In the 70s and early 80s, there wasn't the huge media exposure that there is now. We weren't closeting ourselves from the media, so dressing-rooms were usually a free-for-all for everybody. We never had the dressing-room to ourselves but I see that teams do that now.

We had terrible days in the 70s.

Heartbreaking days. The 1978 Munster final has to be the stand-out disappointing moment of our lives.

We knew we had the handle of everybody.

We could beat Kilkenny in Nowlan Park or in Tulla; we could beat Tipp or Limerick. We knew that the All-Ireland was there for us in 1978… if we could just get over the Cork hurdle. The most regrettable part for us was that we lost the match by two points, but we didn't play.

We just didn't perform. Every sportsperson would say that if you perform to your best and get beaten, you'll accept it in time. But when you know you didn't, you'll never accept it.

We were down a point at half-time, having played against the breeze. We knew in our hearts that there was nobody else. There was nothing in Leinster that held any fear for us that time. The winners had Antrim in an All-Ireland semi-final. That was the galling thing about it. It finished up Cork vs Wexford in the final and there was a 12 or 15-point gap.

Facing out for the second-half, here was the 30 minutes that were going to define us as characters and as a team. We had come a long way in four years… and here we were. It just never took off. We were even hoping that Cork would get a goal.

If they had, it might have lifted the lid off the match, but it just didn't happen. It has always been very hard to accept that… but a lot of us didn't perform. We have to put our hands up. Ger Loughnane and Seamus Durack performed, but an awful lot of us just didn't.

I was terrible. Dreadful.

We were marking men instead of going out and expressing ourselves. In his autobiography, John Callinan put his finger on it. Justin McCarthy was marvellous but his lead-up to the match was about how to *stop* Cork. We went out to stop Cork and we didn't go out and just play. We were every bit as good as them, if not better.

We allowed ourselves to be led, rather than going out and us all being leaders. I could go on about that forever... but people are sick and tired of hearing that song.

That said, we'd like to think that we were ground-breakers. We won the two National Leagues. We were the fairytale team really and we had a massive following. Sometimes you wouldn't know who'd be togging out in the dressing-room, there were so many in there. They were marvellous times. It's a different era now and they don't have that same fun.

In 1983, we played Cork in the league on a Sunday and we played the county final on the Monday. The following Saturday, we played the Munster club game down in Midleton. The referee took the match off us.

We got a goal and went two points ahead in the 30th minute of the second-half. The puck-out was taken and play was going on. The next thing... an umpire put up his hand, the referee went in and disallowed the goal... and Midleton won it.

They finished up in the All-Ireland final.

We had a huge Oireachtas final against Kilkenny the following day in Ennis. Whatever clicked on the Saturday, we had five bus-loads of Sixmilebridge people in Midleton.

After getting beaten, the usual happened, we took the long journey home. Fr O'Dowd was driving me and Tom Quinn (RIP), who lived and died for the club all his life.

We drank our sorrows on the way home. Fr O'Dowd brought me within a mile of my house. I said I was up the road a bit further.

'I know where you live,' he said. It was about four in the morning, it was raining hard and I asked him would he run me up?

'I will not!' he said. 'You need to walk off those 10 pints that you're after drinking. You're playing Kilkenny tomorrow.'

The following day, the first four Kilkenny players that got out of a Fiesta parked beside me in the Quinnsworth car park, as it was that time, were Ger Henderson, John Henderson, Frank Cummins, and Dick O'Hara. Four animals of men.

The fiesta lifted about a foot and a half off the ground when they got out. I looked out the window and thought... *How am I going to face them after 10 pints and three matches in the one week?*

I came out after the match with the Man of the Match trophy in my hand. Fr O'Dowd was standing at the back of the stand, with Fr Seamus Gardiner and the future Bishop, Willie Walsh.

I said to Fr O'Dowd, 'What did you think of that?'

We had won by a point. He said, 'I've lost all faith. It makes no sense.' It was one of those days; if I had gone up into the press box, the ball would have followed me.

I meet Jackie O'Gorman and we'd be talking about the teams who won in 1995, '97 and 2013 and I'd be saying, 'Isn't it great what they did'.

He'd be saying, 'It's marvellous… but they were having no fun. We probably had too much of it'.

When I look back at the record of Cork teams in the 70s; they won All-Ireland minors and under-21s. They created a super senior team that won three All-Irelands in-a-row, when we were at our peak. They were our nemesis.

I'm not demeaning any of Clare's All-Irelands since. 1997 was the one because they beat Tipperary twice but in '95, the super powers were at their weakest. Take Tipp, Kilkenny and Cork out of the equation and you'd fancy your chances every day of the week.

I always loved running and I still run.

I discovered that late because I wasn't physically very strong. I knew that I wasn't physically strong, compared to the likes of Frank Cummins and Timmy Crowley. You had to try to out-think them a small bit and have more stamina than them. I was 27 or 28 when I discovered that I had better start putting in the mileage because I needed something that the rest of them hadn't got.

Tim Crowe asked me lately was I still running? I told him I was just after coming back from a 10km run. He understands it; he was a runner himself.

'It's a drug!' he said and I said, 'Definitely!'

You could be halfway through a 10km run and you're suddenly a different person once you clean out the pipes.

That would be my advice to most players; try to get a handle on what you're best at in order to counteract your weak points. Pace is temporary, but stamina lasts a long time. That's why I love to put stamina into lads… but a lot of coaches don't adhere to that.

A huge pinnacle would have been watching the team of the 90s doing what they did. They played with no fear of anybody. They didn't work any harder than we worked but they expressed themselves every day, especially in the 1995 All-Ireland semi-final against Galway. They just tore at them and they didn't care if they made mistakes.

We were always fearful of doing the right thing and of not making mistakes.

I still love hurling with a passion and I can never leave it.

I'd meet cohorts of mine, who won four or five championships here in Sixmilebridge and I'd ask them do they miss it? A few of them would say, 'Not one bit. I don't miss the hassle of training'.

Some fellas just hated training, but I loved training more than matches, because at training you had no fear of doing something wrong.

I love hurling more now than I ever did.

I love the scent of the dressing-room and being around the game. It's the kick you get out of it… the friendships and the memories.

TOMMY KEANE

KILMALEY 0-10 ÉIRE ÓG 0-8
Clare SHC Final
Cusack Park
SEPTEMBER 8, 1985

Overcoming Éire Óg to help Kilmaley claim their first Senior Championship title is a day that remains with Tommy Keane more than any of the great days he spent on duty with Clare.

★ **KILMALEY:** PJ Kennedy; M Darcy, N McGuane, P Hill; P Keane, **T Keane**, N Romer; E McMahon, M Cahill; S Fitzpatrick (0-3), G Pyne, M Meehan (0-3); J Cahill, J Mungovan, G Kennedy (0-3). Subs: M Murphy (0-1) for J Cahill, M Killeen for Pyne.

★ **ÉIRE ÓG:** S Durack; M Meagher, P Kelly, G Barry; J Russell (0-1), M Glynn, P Mahon; D Coote (0-3), M O'Sullivan; P Lynch, S Heaslip (0-3), G Mannion; B O'Brien (0-1), N Ryan, M Nugent. Subs: S McCarthy for Mahon, M Ryan for O'Sullivan, P Barry for O'Brien.

THE ACTION

ANY CLUB LUCKY enough to win a senior championship or two remembers their first one. Kilmaley certainly do.

High scoring it wasn't but the 1985 Clare senior final was not short of passion, emotion and drama. Led by their goalkeeping captain PJ Kennedy, Kilmaley showed all of their fight, grit and tenacity on the big day. And, Kennedy made a crucial early save when denying Pa Lynch a goal. Kilmaley also displayed an astuteness on the sideline, which played a central role in helping them to glory.

Tommy Keane had been enjoying a superb championship at centre-back but Kilmaley switched their county man with corner-back Paddy Hill in the first-half, and both players benefited immensely. Hill excelled at centre-back, while Keane mopped up a lot of possession in the Kilmaley full-back line.

The sides were tied 0-4 each at half-time, following an industrious first-half. The hurling didn't flow but every score was earned. Early in the second-half, Kilmaley's Martin Meehan pointed twice before Seamie Fitzpatrick and Meehan again added to their side's tally. Kilmaley now led 0-8 to 0-4 and they had one hand on the Canon Hamilton Cup.

Éire Óg didn't lie down, though, and points from Bernie O'Brien and Declan Coote brought them back into it. John Russell added to Éire Óg's tally before Kilmaley substitute Michael Murphy pointed. This was added to by a pointed Gerry Kennedy free and Kilmaley were on the cusp.

Very late in the game, Seán Heaslip went for goal from a close-in dead ball but the shot was repelled.

Kilmaley were champions for the first time and their joy was unrelenting. They had taken down the mighty Éire Óg, who had started as understandably warm favourites.

★ ★ ★ ★ ★

66

I WAS INVOLVED with the county at the time and I was summonsed back to the club for a training session of a Saturday evening in the middle of the summer. The first thing that struck me was the fitness of some of the lads, and how they had changed in two months.

Noel McGuane had lost about three stone. I asked him what was he at? He said he had gone up into the forestry, where nobody could see him and he had trained every evening. He got himself back into shape, and back into the team. I don't think he was on the team at the start of the championship but he ended up probably the best full-back in the county that year.

When I look back on it, 1985 was definitely the highlight. I don't think we won a game in 1984.

I don't think much about defeats and I don't want to be recalling them either.

There was a change of management when Jim McMahon and Brian O'Reilly came in; the whole thing changed. We had the players alright. We had won a minor and two under-21 Championships. We had them, but it was all about getting it together and getting everyone to commit.

The two boys, Jim and Brian, had a huge influence. When Jim talked, you'd listen. If he had something to say, he always took you aside. He never ridiculed anyone in front of the group. He'd take you aside and give you a fair lecture then. We all got it... myself included. You would listen to him though, and you took it on board. He had a great way about him.

In the league section of the championship, Newmarket were leading us by 12 points in the second-half but we came back to beat them. I know they were gone a bit off the boil a bit, but they still had a lot of great hurlers.

Willie Pyne got married the day before the quarter-final. Half the team were at the wedding but they looked after themselves well. We beat the 'Mills and that set us up for the 'Bridge in the semi-final. They were Munster club champions at the time.

The 'Bridge were raging hot favourites and we drew with them in a game we should have won. We were told we had no business turning up the second day; that we had got our chance and we hadn't taken it.

I remember one of the Éire Óg lads saying to me, when we were coming out, that we'd never again get the chance. But we went in the following week and we beat them. We held them to five points from play… 1-5 was all they scored and the goal came in the last minute. We beat them well the same evening.

We were way better than them. We learned more from the drawn game than they had, or else the 'Bridge thought it was a once-off and it wasn't going to happen a second time.

The game was on a Sunday evening and we had a few pucks on the Saturday evening. I never saw lads in such a positive frame of mind.

Another thing came into play then. The county final was to be played in Carron. It had been due to be played there the year before for Centenary Year but it wasn't ready. It was an awful bad summer that year… rain, rain, rain. We went to Carron one evening to train, a week or 10 days before the final. Conditions up there were bad.

Éire Óg didn't want to go to Carron. They were afraid of us, I'd say, in a tight field.

It was changed back to Cusack Park.

It was all the same. We'd have them beaten wherever it was played. It was a great achievement, given where we had come from.

I saw people at that final and maybe for a week after, that I didn't think even knew we played hurling. The whole parish got involved. There was no-one left at home. It was awful uplifting, especially with the bad year. Being a rural parish, with a bad summer… maybe no hay, bad silage and no turf… it was a real lift.

We came back out to Kilmaley that night and the whole county was there. There were lads there from everywhere. I think we even put Marty Morrissey in the picture. I remember doing an interview with him after the game. He was only starting out. Aidan Tuttle used to do the commentary that time.

We probably went into the final under a bit more pressure. I felt more pressure in the final anyway. I had played well in a couple of the games before that and maybe I put a lot of pressure on myself.

Lads had been saying to me that I had to play well. Probably the worst game I had in the championship was in the county final. But we had heaps of good hurlers.

We had a serious defence and we had Martin Meehan and Seamie Fitz up front, two inter-county lads. We had Niall Romer... and my brother Pat was in the team as well. Martin Cahill had a fine game that day. The bulk of the team had come from under-14 up along.

There was no panic in any game. The thing was totally calm. Jim did the bit of talking but there was no pressure. The dressing-room was awful relaxed but very focused. I'd put that down to Brian O'Reilly and Jim McMahon.

A lot of us had never known what it was like to be fit. A lot of the lads would drink porter and go out and play a match. That's what was happening.

We were getting away with it up along. We won the intermediate in 1980 and went senior the following year. We won the Clare Cup after going up, but then we had a couple of awful bad years.

We weren't good enough the way we were carrying on but we had plenty of hurlers. We just weren't prepared properly for senior hurling and there were a lot of good teams around. It was a big step up from intermediate.

The Munster final was on the first Sunday in July that time and that was as far as Clare ever went. Club championship then started after that. You also knew when the championship was going to be played.

As regards a routine, in the lead-up to a match, the evening before, I'd get someone to puck balls to me for 15 minutes. I'd even go into a shed and belt a few balls against a wall to get my eye in. We all went to the match our own way. For that county final, myself and Pat went in.

There was no get-together before the match. It was straight into the dressing-room and out.

We'd get the team on the day of the game but you'd know the team from the way it was lined out at training. We won that championship using 18 or 19 players.

The team was set and we didn't have any serious injuries. We were a hardy crew that time. A lot of us were from farms and were used to forking bales and working in the bog. Although I spent the whole of 1982 out with a hamstring, we had very little of those things, aside from a few bruises.

These days, players' bodies are being wrecked from training.

Maybe we should have won one or two more after that. We played five and a half hours with Clarecastle in the semi-final two years after and it ended up that there was only a point between us.

1986 was very flat. We were still celebrating '85. We put it together again in 1987 and had a right good run. After that, it kind of went downhill.

The longer it went on, the more 1985 meant. At the time, we were still playing and maybe we didn't think that much about it.

There are probably some of the lads I haven't met since the 25th anniversary presentation at the 2010 county final. Johnsy Mungovan is in Boston; he went soon after 1985 and I think he only came home once. He was full-forward on that team. Paddy Hill is a man I wouldn't meet too often either; he's down in Cork.

Most of the rest of them are local or aren't gone too far. I'd meet a lot of them at Kilmaley matches. We'd be in contact all the time. When you look at the present Kilmaley team, the bulk of them are local. We really haven't got anyone in.

We played Blackrock in the Munster club. They had the Cashmans, Dermot McCurtain and Eamon O'Donoghue. They beat us in Cusack Park. We weren't as focused and, on the day, we weren't good enough. We met a good team.

I came in with the county in 1977 after Clare won the first league. I was there or thereabouts until 1987, although '86 really finished me with the county. I was captain that year and we lost a Munster final that we definitely should have won. I looked at it, for the first time, last Christmas (2020). I nearly got sick again looking at it.

We were probably the better team that day. We were up a couple of points at half-time. I remember James Shanahan got a ball, about 40 yards out in front of the goal, to level it. He mishit it. It went in low and it was cleared. They came down and got a point out of it.

I should have hooked one of the Cork players for one of their goals. I'll never forget it. We made a few small mistakes but I still think we should have won it. All we needed that time was a small break, but we never seemed to get it.

In the 1981 Munster final, only for Joe McKenna, we could have won it. I think it was bad management in that Jim Power was playing serious hurling and he was always able to mark McKenna. McKenna got 3-3 the same day. They never made a change. I was corner-back... Barry Smythe and myself were in the two corners.

Looking at the way players train now, I wouldn't hurl at all.

They're wrecking them. The fun is gone out of it.

You'd want a 9 to 5 job. Once they hit 27 or 28 now, they seem to be gone for various reasons. We trained hard and we minded ourselves at the weekend, but we went out to hurl for the craic.

After every one of those games in 1985, there was a big session on the Sunday night… and maybe on the Monday. Then we were back training again on the Tuesday. It didn't do a thing to us. Now it's into an ice bath you're going after playing a match… and you mightn't have a game again for three weeks.

These rucks in hurling, I can't stand them. In our time, if there was a ruck like that, there would be four ankles broken before someone would come out of it. If a fella pulls overhead now, there's a free given against him.

It's all about possession, running and hand-passing it. It's gone like football, running with it and throwing it to a fella running alongside you… someone might hit it eventually.

Another thing that has it ruined is the sweeper.

One time it was man-to-man and if your man got inside you, more than likely it was a goal. Now if he gets inside you, he has two or three more to beat.

It's killing good forwards.

I nearly prefer now to watch the Kilmaley under-15 or under-16 teams than watch a senior team playing.

Maybe I'm raving but that's the way I see it.

99

TOMMY GUILFOYLE

FEAKLE 1-17 RUAN 1-10
Clare SHC Final
Cusack Park
SEPTEMBER 11, 1988

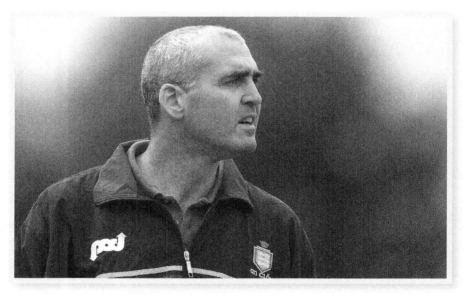

Ten years of hard work by so many great people led to Feakle finally landing the Clare Senior Championship title in 1988, and giving Tommy Guilfoyle a day to always remember.

★ **FEAKLE:** G McNamara; G Loughnane, S McGrath, M Hogan; E Slattery, P Callinan, J Tuohy 'Dromore'; H McMahon, D McGrath; M Daly, V Donnellan (0-7), B Slattery (0-1); M Callinan (0-2), **T Guilfoyle (0-1)**, M Guilfoyle (1-5). Subs: J Guilfoyle for P Callinan, J Tuohy 'Gurrane' (0-1) for M Daly.

★ **RUAN:** K McDonnell; G Lyons, J Moroney, J Courtney; M Moroney, C Lyons (0-6), F Lyons; A Meaney, M Moroney; S O'Loughlin, T Kelly (0-1), K O'Brien; M Daffy (0-3), D Hassett, S O'Donoghue. Subs: D Mulqueen for A Meaney, PJ Lyons (1-0) for K O'Brien.

THE ACTION

WHEN REFEREE MICHAEL Quinn sounded the long whistle in Cusack Park as the clock ticked towards 5pm, 44 years had passed since Feakle last called themselves Clare senior hurling champions. Their joy was uproarious and unrelenting.

Twelve months earlier, they had finished four points adrift of Clarecastle (0-15 to 0-11) in that year's final. In winning that one and nailing down two in-a-row, Clarecastle avenged their 1939 loss to Feakle, who completed three in-a-row in 1940.

The men from the tranquil East Clare village won their sixth Senior Championship in that 1988 final guided by a management team of Tony Hayes, Paddy Minogue, Fr Harry Bohan, and Ger Loughnane, who doubled as player/coach.

In front of a county final crowd of almost 10,000 people, they bridged a gap stretching back to 1944, when they won their fifth championship. Feakle were captained by Val Donnellan, who finished the year as championship top scorer, with a total of 3-35.

Ruan, who were inspired by full-back John Moroney and centre-back Cyril Lyons, led by a point at half-time, 0-7 to 0-6. They had to start without the injured PJ Lyons, who came on as a sub and scored a goal, while Eddie Casey was laid up with 'flu.

Michael Guilfoyle put away Feakle's goal early in the second-half, set up by a pass from his brother Tommy. Michael Guilfoyle scored a total of 1-5 in a Man of the Match performance.

Feakle were leading by three points entering the last 15 minutes, when their goalkeeper, Ger McNamara made a crucial intervention as Ruan full-forward Donal Hassett hit a goal-bound shot.

From there on, Feakle sensed that the day was theirs and they hit six successive points to establish an unassailable lead. PJ Lyons netted for Ruan in the closing minutes but the day and the year belonged to Feakle.

After years of underage success, which included winning four successive under-21A titles, a generation of hurlers had finally clasped their hands on the Canon Hamilton Cup.

★ ★ ★ ★ ★

"

THERE WERE ELDERLY men crying in the dressing-room, and lads had brought naggins of whiskey and brandy in and they were passing them around.

Nowadays, there would be stewards keeping supporters off the field and there would be no-one allowed into the tunnel. That was of the time. It probably wouldn't be seen as the right thing to do now but, at that stage, no-one cared.

I marked the late John Moroney that day. We used to mark each other at Clare training in 1985, '86 and '87. I used to hate going to training but I knew if I could play on John Moroney, I could play against anyone.

He was full-back for Ruan and he kept me fairly quiet. I got one lucky break; I caught a ball over his head and passed it to Michael [Guilfoyle] for the goal. We didn't have any baggage with Ruan. Maybe if it had been Clarecastle or Sixmilebridge, we would have been under more pressure.

It's in the past now, but some things come back to you.

There was a massive crowd for two small parishes. We beat Clooney-Quin in the first round, then Tubber/Crusheen by two points and Scariff in the quarter-final, our neighbours from six miles down the road. We won that 0-18 to 2-2… then we beat Éire Óg 2-11 to 2-8 in the semi-final.

We would have had no fear of Ruan. We were down 0-7 to 0-6 at half-time but we won it by seven points in the end.

(Ger) Loughnane had instilled confidence in everyone. He had convinced the corner-backs, for example, that they could take on anyone and they believed him.

Anytime we won anything, we always had to stop at Miko's Cross. We had Smythe's lorry and as many as could get on the lorry, hopped on. The lorry used to bring stones from McGrath's quarry or turf from the Bog of Allen.

Men, women and children were in the parade with one of the Tulla piper's leading it. We'd congregate and then we'd do *the tour* of the village.

That's still done to this day.

Feakle isn't a big place; there are no bypasses or anything. We'd go over to Pepper's Pub by the graveyard, back around by the hotel and the school. Depending on who was at the front, we'd go around a couple of times.

There's a small pub outside Feakle, Mickey Naughton's. I'd say you could probably fit 10 into it. The sing-song went on all night.

There was probably a bigger build-up to the 1987 final, when we lost to Clarecastle, because we hadn't been there since '58.

We would have heard of teams in the late 30s and early 40s, when they won three in-a-row. They had some outstanding hurlers, who went on to play for Clare and Munster but that was in the past.

Our team wasn't held down by tradition because we just hadn't been successful. We set about being successful at underage and eventually we got our big day out in 1988 after losing the year before.

Then we had the Munster club journey.

We were drawn against Ballyduff from Kerry in the first round. Probably the small regret we have, to this day, is that we lost the semi-final to Mount Sion.

We had a team that was known for high scoring. We had good forwards but the score that day was 1-8 to 1-7. Val Donnellan would have got 1-7 every day. It was a wet, windy day and Val got an asthmatic attack that week. In the final, we would have come up against Patrickswell and it was a case of what could have been.

We won one championship but we should have and could have won more. We won one... but how precious it was.

We used to have 15 to 20 elderly men come to the field every evening for training. It was a social outing and they might go for a few pints up the street after.

I remember MP Loughnane, a legendary Feakle hurler. It was always said that he never let a puck-out fall to the ground, that he could double on every puck-out... and he wasn't a big man. He used to come over with people like James Moloney, John Anglim and Paudie Nugent. He was a Dub who came to Feakle. The rural housing is beside the hurling field.

People who had emigrated came back in 1988 from America and England. Probably one of our best supporters was John Joe Naughton, who used to come back from New York for as many matches as he could. John Joe bought a car the first time he came.

He left it at his aunt's place; so when he came home he always had a car. Whether it was taxed or insured was another thing! The players really appreciated that someone made the effort to come home from New York. After the county final, John Joe didn't want to go back, but he had to. He played for Feakle in the

50s or 60s. There was a legendary game where he scored four or five goals. It was always told in the pub.

We were lucky, because there was a lot of emigration in the 80s. I can't remember any of my crowd that went to college. You either did an apprenticeship, or you got a job in a factory. Or you probably stayed at home on the family farm. College wasn't the thing, nor was travel.

Travel that time was a one-way ticket. Our lads would have been prepared to work at anything. I was lucky. I got a job with De Beers (now Element Six) in Shannon in 1983 and I'm still there 38 years on.

It culminated in 1988, but the seeds were sown when a group of people got together and organised the underage. We had been coming. We won three Clare Cups (Division 1 league) in the space of five or six years and we lost three of four finals as well. The reason it was special to me was because it wasn't an overnight success.

It was based on 10 years of work from 1979 onwards.

In a rural club like Feakle, you make hay while the sun shines… when you have the players. In 1979 we won under-14 B and under-16 B titles. We progressed up the grades and won under-16 and minor A. Then we won four under-21 As and were beaten in the fifth final. I captained the team for the fifth one; the one we lost, as usual. That was the norm of the day. Any team that I captained always lost.

I remember one of the junior B's we won, when I was in my late-forties; they made me captain. That was in 2010. In my acceptance speech, I said that it was the first time I had ever won anything as captain.

The manager jumped in and said, 'If I knew that, you wouldn't have been captain!' We won the junior B with 12 of the panel that won the county final in 1988.

Subsequent to 1988, we went into free-fall. We were relegated to intermediate and our underage numbers were very low. Sometime in the early 80s, Ger Loughnane transferred away from us to Wolfe Tones (Shannon). When Loughnane transferred away, there was a lot of disappointment in Feakle.

Two of our best players had transferred. Seamus Durack had gone to Éire Óg… and now Loughanne had gone.

After a league game against Kilkenny, myself, Michael and Val Donnellan were in the West County Hotel in Ennis. Fr Harry was a selector with Clare at the time. It was late-1986, I think.

We were standing in the bar chatting and Fr Harry threw it out to Loughnane. He said, 'You might come back to us?' Loughnane said he would. We didn't believe him, but he did come back and he took over the coaching of the team.

I think he sensed that we had a chance of winning a championship, based on our underage success. He always puts down winning that championship as one of his favourite days.

Fr Harry was involved in the management. We were lucky in that we had the players, and we probably had the best coach in Ireland; and we had the best man-manager in Fr Harry.

1988 was also special in that my father Tommy was the chairman. My mother washed all the jerseys from under-12s to the seniors. Michael got Man of the Match in that county final and my younger brother John came on as a substitute for Paul Callinan, who had got injured. It was a real family occasion.

Paddy Minogue was our director of hurling. The year we won the intermediate, a couple of years ago, Paddy tragically passed away. No more than we heard about people in the 40s and 50s, the current team would have heard of Paddy Minogue. I remember the night of the medal presentation in 1988, he stated that he didn't coach from a textbook, that he coached from the 'Handbook of Life'. That meant loyalty, commitment and pride.

If Paddy Minogue called training at 4pm, everyone was there because Paddy was a busy man. He was self-employed. He was involved with those under-21 teams and some of those campaigns would have gone late into the year. Lads would have got off work to train, while it was bright.

We grew up together, we won together and we stuck together.

There are a lot of lads on the current Feakle senior team, who are sons of lads who played on our team. There's still a connection there.

There were 12 sets of brothers on the '88 panel. You had the Slatterys, McMahons, Callinans, Tuohys, Donnellans, Hogans and Guilfoyles. We won the Junior A Championship as well in 1988. We nearly always had 34 or 35 at training.

Unfortunately, some of those players have passed away. Con McGuinness passed away in his forties from a heart attack. We had two John Tuohys... Garraun and Dromore. That's the way they were always named in *The Clare Champion*. John passed away in his thirties and Seán Tobin, who trained with us, passed away at a young age too.

We had a lot of good people involved in the club as officers in the 70s and 80s. During that era, we were blessed to have an outsider come in who became one of our own. Michael Lillis was from Patrickswell in Limerick.

He came to Feakle as a forester. He used to work with Noel Lane in South Galway and East Clare. He was a great guy and I would have put my house on him becoming the president of the GAA.

I remember the great Aidan Tuttle said that he was wasting his time because no-one as intelligent as him should be allowed into a Clare County Board meeting. The great 'Tut' said that.

Michael moved after he got a big job in Dublin. His administration skills were above anything that I would ever have seen. He came from a forest in East Clare to the head office of Coillte in Dublin.

His motto, as chairman or secretary, was that with any problem that arose, a good administrator should see it and cut it off. He got involved with Blackhall Gaels in Meath. Between Feakle and Patrickswell, football wouldn't have been too high on the list. He was a brilliant man. When he left Feakle, it was like a death in the family. He left about four or five years after 1988.

I mentioned about all the brothers that were involved, but it was a way of life in Feakle for the mothers and fathers too. This journey started in 1979. Parents were involved then and right up to 2010, when we won the junior B. I think it was my mother's 70th birthday that night. We were 10 points down at half-time and Clooney were organising the victory parade.

We just somehow pulled it out of the bag; talk about a Dad's Army. It was a big family occasion because all our sons and daughters were at it. We made the usual stop in John Minogue's in Tulla. John is a Tulla man but he's really a Feakle man.

Clare-wise, I had a particularly good game in the 1986 Munster final in Killarney against Cork. It was one of those days when we probably should have won but probably didn't believe that we could. I'd still meet people who talk about that weekend.

Another highlight, prior to winning the championship in 1988, was when we were the only Clare club that won the All-Ireland seven-a-side. We got beaten in 1985 by Glen Rovers from Cork early in the day. We then played Glen Rovers again in the final. We had played Patrickswell, Kinnity and a London team, who had Mickey Burke from Whitegate.

We had the forwards, although ironically Val used to play in the backs. He used to puck it out to me and I'd pass it to Michael. That was the set move.

When word filtered through to Feakle that we were in the final, there were people who got into their cars at 3pm that day and drove to Dublin. The night we won, we were so shattered, we weren't able to go out. One guy thought he knew the Dublin Bus system and we got lost in the middle of the city.

The great Jimmy Lynch (RIP) was the manager. He was an uncle of Colin Lynch. If there was a wall to be built, a roof to be fixed or a back netting to be taken down, Jimmy was there. We used to affectionately call him The Taoiseach because he was involved in everything.

When Feakle won the intermediate in 2014, myself and Killian Bane, the captain, lifted him out of his wheelchair and he presented the cup. He has died since. Someone said a miracle happened that day. He went into Cusack Park in a wheelchair and he walked out. He had been in hospital that week. He was a legend in Feakle. Men like him are what really make the GAA special. People like Michael Lillis and Paddy Minogue all did their bit and more.

We also had a famous man called Tony Tuohy. He was known as The Boxer. He used to keep the score either on the inside of a Major fag box or on the base of a hurley. On one of the nights we won the under-21, he fell into the bonfire. He was wearing a white Aran jumper but it came out black.

One memory from 1988 that has always stuck in my mind, was when we were in Bohan's pub. Myself, Fr Harry and Micheál Bohan (Fr Harry's brother); it was about 4am and we were sitting on high stools.

I never really drank but I'd had a couple of brandies.

We were all talked-out and we looked at one another.

This was heaven and we knew it. There was nothing left to say.

99

DAVID FORDE

SCARIFF COMMUNITY COLLEGE 2-12
ST FLANNAN'S COLLEGE, ENNIS 0-7
Dean Ryan Final
Gaelic Grounds Limerick
DECEMBER 7, 1990

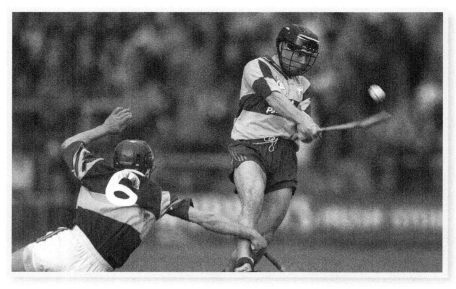

The epic 'David and Goliath' nature of defeating St Flannan's in 1990 made the victory all the sweeter for David Forde.

★ **SCARIFF COMMUNITY COLLEGE:** J Ryan; J Cleary, G Collins, P Boland; S Brett (0-1), B Minogue (0-1), PJ Vaughan; D Kelly, T Nugent (1-0); B Murphy (1-3), **D Forde (0-1)**, D Tuohy (0-4); O Sheedy (0-1), G McNamara, E Murphy. Subs: A Ward for Vaughan, C Ryan (0-1) for E Murphy, B McInerney for McNamara.

★ **ST FLANNAN'S COLLEGE:** D Scanlan; B Quinn, J Collins, D Hoey; R Burke, R Woods, J Considine; R O'Hara, O Baker; N Tuohy, F Hegarty (0-1), K Morrissey; B Tobin (0-3), J Healy (0-3), T Fahy. Subs: M McLoughlin for Considine, M Conlon for McLoughlin.

THE ACTION

FOR THE FIRST time, a team from the East Clare school had qualified for a Munster A colleges final. In their way was a giant of second-level hurling in the province who, at that stage, had already annexed seven Dean Ryan titles. Scariff Community College were given absolutely no chance of shocking St Flannan's.

While the Clare hurling public might have believed that Scariff's best hope was to maybe compete, the Diarmuid Tuohy-captained team had more belief than that. They saw it as an opportunity to show what they could do and they delivered in spectacular fashion.

That showed in the way they started. They fired over three early points from Tuohy, Brian Minogue and future Clare senior Barry Murphy. The Scariff man netted their first-half goal and come the interval they led 1-8 to 0-5. A sensation was on the cards.

St Flannan's had moved full-forward James Healy to midfield in an effort to establish a foothold in the opening half. The Ennis school had considerably upped their game before half-time but they couldn't reel in Scariff Community College. However, they were floored in the second-half when a long Owen Sheedy delivery was deflected to the St Flannan's net.

St Flannan's did not add to their total in the last 22 minutes, although they had opportunities to do so.

Scariff Community College sensed that their moment had come and they played very intelligent hurling to see out the game. When the final whistle was heard at the Gaelic Grounds, it signalled absolute ecstasy for the Scariff players, mentors and their supporters in the crowd of approximately 3,000 people.

★ ★ ★ ★ ★

66

WE WERE THE small guys taking on the big boys.

When you'd look back on it, we were coming from clubs that played C hurling. My club Ogonnelloe played C hurling… so did Bodyke, Feakle, Broadford, Killanena and O'Callaghan's Mills.

Whitegate and Scariff probably bucked the trend, in that they were playing A or B. We were the minnows going into the Gaelic Grounds in Limerick to play St Flannan's.

At the time, it was magic. I can still remember the game and I can still remember the week or two afterwards. The school went mental. That was the time when all of the school would have gone to the match. We had about 600 pupils… everyone was there.

St Flannan's had an unbelievable team. They had Ollie Baker and Fergal Hegarty… Richard Woods was centre-back… Danny Scanlon was in goals… James Healy was full-forward and Terence Fahy from Whitegate was corner-forward.

David Hoey, Ronan O'Hara and Niall Tuohy were also playing. A lot of those guys went on to play county.

The scoreline isn't a good reflection on the game; it was a lot tighter than that. Johnny Ryan from Bodyke was our goalkeeper and he made some unbelievable saves. They got a man sent off as well.

I started secondary school in Scariff in 1990. That year Scariff won the Munster Senior B. By winning the Senior B, that put us into the A competitions for the following year. That allowed us to enter the Dean Ryan and the Harty Cup. I was in second year when we entered the Dean Ryan.

We played Coláiste Chríost Rí in the first round and we won well… and then North Monastery in the quarter-final and got through that.

In the semi-final, it was tight against Limerick CBS, and there was a bit of controversy. There was a free late in the game that was waved wide and we got the benefit of it. We got a point at the end to win it.

Then it was St Flannan's in the final.

Whatever about the other schools, Flannan's was the big one. They had won the Harty Cup in 1990 and in '91. They were big news. The feeling was that if you wanted to play hurling, you'd have to go to St Flannan's.

I was centre-forward and I played all right. I got a point but I don't think I was brilliant. Stephen Brett was brilliant and Johnny Ryan kept us in it with those great saves. The other brilliant thing about it was that every club in East Clare had a player on the team and the panel; Feakle and Scariff had a good few but everyone else had one or two.

When you look back on it now, it was unbelievable.

There was no big plan. We just went out and hurled. I can't remember many tactics but there weren't many at that time anyway. PJ Mason was over the team with John Kelly, who was the school principal. There was a guy called Vincent Teehan from Offaly, who was the equivalent of an East Clare coach. He would come into the school and he used to train teams. He'd be a selector on the team and he was excellent.

There was no first year hurling at that time, so your first introduction to hurling would have been in second year. A few of us played Tony Forristal hurling in the summer with Clare. For John Cleary, PJ Vaughan, Alan Ward and myself, that was our introduction to county hurling. We were then brought into the Dean Ryan squad at school.

We'd get Des Hassett's bus to the match. He had a pub in Tuamgraney. The day of the final, we stopped in Broadford… had a walk in the wood. Afterwards, we went back to the school and we had a big stew in the Home Economics room. It was simple stuff but very enjoyable.

Only two of our team went on to play senior inter-county; Barry Murphy and myself. A lot of our lads could have played county but it wasn't the culture at that time. The vast majority of lads went working straight away after they finished up at school. That was an East Clare thing. You went off and went working.

We never made any inroads in Harty Cup afterwards. For example, Diarmuid Tuohy was captain but he was in Leaving Cert. He could have played two more years of Harty but he was gone.

Scariff won the Dean Ryan again in 1996 but, since then, the school has been playing C and D hurling. There was a great influx of lads that time and it coincided with Clare going well. Population-wise, there were a lot of us and I'd say the population went down after that. There were 120 in my year.

I often found, when we played in the under-16 Nenagh Co-op competition, East Clare used to do really well. But when we went into the county, we were nearly intimidated by A club players, thinking they were better than us. They weren't but in our own heads, they were… and we felt that they looked down on us. There was an element of that in it.

I was stone mad for hurling. I wanted to make it.

I did a lot of training myself, and was hugely motivated to play for Clare.

Getting the ball in the 1997 Munster final against Tipperary, I remember thinking… *I'll put it over the bar.* I think fate put it in the net for me. Sparrow (Ger O'Loughlin) tried to flick it over the corner-back's head. I came across and collected it.

It was definitely written in the stars for me. I've taken a lot of shots but I never hit a goal like that; in under the crossbar. It was meant for me.

When you're hurling, you do a lot of that stuff automatically. If you thought about it, the moment would be gone. You get the ball into your hands, you go a few steps and you hit it. You don't really think about it too much.

The crowd were on top of us and the noise was unbelievable.

I remember the feeling I had… it was numbness. I remember Fergie Tuohy coming over to me and saying to keep the head and to keep it going.

It was surreal in ways. The noise running out… not really knowing what was going on.

Then when it's all over, you go back and play with your club. You're not the big guy any more, unless you prove it again. You'll be playing against fellas trying to cut you down to size.

But I loved playing club hurling.

I've great memories of league and championship games. We were quite successful. We had good players and you weren't on your own. If you weren't playing well, there was always one or two others that would pull you through. I suppose our problem was that we didn't have enough. We probably needed one or two more players; one or two more, and we could have done another bit.

We played Wolfe Tones in 1998 and there was nine minutes of injury time played. Players wouldn't notice or realise it. You'd just keep playing. Wolfe Tones won the first game with a very late goal but it was refixed and that went to extra time. It was a draw again… they won the third game.

The year after that, we drew with Doora-Barefield. We should have won that game. They were after winning the All-Ireland club. We were very close, but we just couldn't get beyond that.

That Dean Ryan final is the one that I still remember very fondly.

We started like rockets. There was no fear. Flannan's had the fear. I'd say that was the problem for them more than us. They couldn't bear losing to us… whereas we had nothing to lose. I'd say if we played them again, they'd beat us. Why wouldn't they, with the players they had!

They were only young lads too. Maybe in their own heads they felt that they should have been better than us. When they weren't then, the pressure really told.

It's a shame in some ways that it hasn't been marked. It'll be lost in another 30 years.

We'll be all old men then!

99

OLLIE BAKER

CLARE 1-17 LAOIS 0-5
National Hurling League Round Five
O'Moore Park, Portlaoise
FEBRUARY 26, 1995

Ollie Baker enjoyed Munster and All-Ireland glory in his first year in 1995 in a Clare senior jersey (above tussling with Cork) but his first start only resulted after he thumbed several lifts to get to the game on time.

★ **CLARE:** D Fitzgerald; M O'Halloran, B Lohan, F Lohan; L Doyle, S McMahon, A Daly (0-1); PJ O'Connell, **O Baker (0-5)**; F Tuohy, C Clancy (0-1), J O'Connor (0-1); C Lyons (0-6), J McInerney (1-1), G O'Loughlin (0-2). Subs: B Quinn for F Lohan, A Neville for O'Connell, E Taaffe for McInerney.

★ **LAOIS:** T Lowry; C Duggan, B Maher, B Dollard; J O'Sullivan, A Bergin, PJ Peacock; O Coss, D Conroy; B McEvoy (0-1), N Delaney (0-1), D Cuddy (0-2); J Bates, O Dowling (0-1), F O'Sullivan. Subs: J Cuddy for Bergin, J Dollard for Bates, J Fitzpatrick for Coss.

THE ACTION

THIRTEEN OF THE Clare starting team against Laois also started the 1995 All-Ireland final on September 3.

On that late-February afternoon in Portlaoise nobody could have foreseen that within a matter of months this group of players and their management team would transform the hurling landscape.

While Laois were nowhere near the top tier at that point, the manner in which Clare eased to victory was perhaps a sign of things to come. They had a settled goalkeeper and six defenders, which became the fulcrum for their double-All-Ireland winning success.

Ken Morrissey had been due to start but he was hit by 'flu. Fergie Tuohy came in at wing-forward, while PJ O'Connell moved to midfield alongside Ollie Baker, who was starting his first game for his county.

Baker made an immediate impact and cut over a lineball from 45 metres out. Cyril Lyons pointed three frees, while Jim McInerney put over the game's first score from open play. Clare completely dominated the half and went in at the interval leading 1-9 to 0-3. McInerney goaled after he was set up by Lyons.

Laois lost David Cuddy early in the second-half when he was sent off and that ended any hope that they might make a game of it. They subsequently added just another solitary point to their tally.

Anthony Daly was the extra man for Clare, who added a flurry of points from Baker, Cyril Lyons, Jamesie O'Connor and Conor Clancy, who had a superb outing.

Clare went on to reach the National League final, where they lost to Kilkenny.

After that game, Ger Loughnane declared that Clare would win the Munster Championship that summer. Nobody knew if he was in earnest or if it was a psychological ploy.

If it was the latter, it definitely paid off.

★★★★★

❝

I HOPPED OUT onto the motorway, beside Bunratty Castle, with the hurleys and gear bag in my hand and stuck out my thumb.

It was a Sunday morning in February of 1995 and I was on my way to Portlaoise, where I was due to start my first league game for Clare.

This game sticks in my memory because my grandmother (Maureen Baker) passed away on the Thursday beforehand. She'd had dementia, so it wasn't a huge shock but of course it was sad for the family.

The team had been named at training on the Thursday night and I was picked to start. I had come on in two games against Galway and Limerick, before Christmas. It was my first year on the panel and this was my first opportunity to get a starting jersey.

These were the days before mobile phones. You generally found out you were named in the starting 15 when it came out in *The Clare Champion* on Thursday.

I had an aunt who was coming over from England, so the funeral Mass was on Sunday morning and we were playing the same day. Ger (Loughnane) and Mike (McNamara) came to the removal and shook hands with everyone. They presumed that when I wasn't there five minutes before the bus was leaving on the Sunday, that I wasn't going to turn up at all.

At home my father had said, 'What are you doing hanging around here? Will you go away and play a game of hurling. There's nothing you can do here anyway. So go on away'.

My timekeeping, generally, is five minutes late. So my uncle Noel dropped me to the West County Hotel.

Bus gone!

I was thinking that they couldn't be gone too long, so the next stop was down in Clarecastle. The uncle drove me to Clarecastle, but they were gone from there too.

The uncle then tore down the road to Newmarket… GONE! The last stop they had in the county was in Bunratty.

My uncle was saying, 'I've to go back to my mother's mass!' He dropped me to Bunratty. Bus gone from there too. There was my starting place gone.

Everything… GONE!

Noel was asking, was I going back with him?

After being told to go to the match by my father, I knew I wasn't going to be welcome at home either. So that's why I had my thumb out, beside Bunratty Castle.

I got a lift, after maybe 20 minutes, to Caherdavin. I put out the thumb again and got a lift to the Nenagh road, at the other side of Limerick city. From there, I got a lift to two or three miles short of Birdhill.

It was getting tight enough at that stage. I had to make up my mind as to whether I was going to continue on. There were 20 minute intervals between every lift.

I had a back-up plan in my mind. I thought that if I got as far as Matt the Thresher's in Birdhill, I'd hang on inside there and listen to the match on the radio and surely someone coming home from the match would give me a lift back to Barefield.

I had all that in my mind and the next thing, a car passed by. They jammed the brakes and reversed back. It was John Casey from Fanore. He was going to the match himself so I said, 'That's great'. The car was full but I was bundled into the back of it.

There were a few questions about why I was late, and I was trying to explain myself. I hadn't known it but the team was stopping at The Racket Hall in Roscrea. I saw the bus as we were passing and I said, 'I'll be grand here'. John jammed again and I got out.

The players and management were coming out to the bus.

All I was afraid of was that they would have named a replacement. Loughnane's face dropped as I came in. It didn't happen too often but he went quiet for a second or two. He said that he was after telling someone that they were starting, I think it was John Chaplin. Loughnane heard the story of how I got there and he said that he couldn't leave me off after that.

They knocked a bit of craic out of it on the bus. I was just 20 years of age and I was as green as grass. You need something like that to bond you with a team. I was the idiot that couldn't make the bus on time.

We went out to play the match and I remember that Sparrow (Ger O'Loughlin) was playing corner-forward. Sparrow always wanted the ball put *into* Sparrow. He didn't want it put in between himself and the corner-back. That wasn't the kind of ball that Sparrow wanted.

He was giving me a bit of guidance going out onto the field and I just felt so comfortable in and around everybody.

We'd had great craic on the bus and I was so relaxed after the panic of getting there.

As it turned out, I scored four points from midfield and a sideline cut. The next time I scored a point from a lineball was in the All-Ireland final. I had a really good game and, in my own mind, I felt completely at home at that level.

The easiest thing to do would have been to stay in the car with my uncle that day and to say that the bus was gone. I don't know would I do it nowadays or would I encourage it. I'd probably have to do 30 laps for missing the bus and I'd have to apologise to the whole panel for letting them down. I'm not sure would it be acceptable these days, but that's the way it was.

Scoring five points gave me a huge boost in confidence. When you're coming in as a young lad, you need some kind of bond with the team to help you feel like you belong there. That takes away all of the doubt that you have about yourself... *Am I good enough to be here?* If you don't have the confidence of the group around you, there's going to be a huge amount of doubt in your own head.

Eight months later, we were walking down the steps of the Hogan Stand with the Liam MacCarthy Cup in our hands. Completely unbelievable and you couldn't plan for it.

In hindsight, you could read a lot into Loughnane starting me against Laois, but I'd say they just said, 'We have to play him after the trouble he went to'.

They were only laughing at the good of it.

That day certainly stuck with me forever, though. When I think of it, I think of nana's anniversary and that maybe she was *Upstairs* looking down, giving me a little bit of comfort and a bit of guidance.

There was nothing made of it at home. I was telling them that I had to get three or four lifts after Noel had dropped me off. The auld lad's answer was, 'Sure, how else were you going to get there?' That's not to bemoan the current generation, although you'd never see a lad out thumbing now. Maybe that is linked to why there is a lack of freedom, for some players, to express themselves on the field. Everything is planned.

There is a huge difference between preparation now compared to back then.

I'd love to say that I was never late again for a game but I can't say that. Still, if we were meeting at 10am tomorrow, I'd be there at five past. There's a more relaxed attitude towards time the further west you go in this country, which I'm okay with.

If management had sat us down in 1995 and said our goal that year was to win the Munster Championship and the All-Ireland, we'd have frozen with the enormity of all of that. They guided us through it game by game.

Loughnane and Mike Mac were doing an awful lot of psychological work, unknown to us. Their genius was to prepare us for when they did come with the pressure; they could say that we had been through all of it. Running out to play in a Munster final in Thurles was never anywhere near as hard as the training we did in Ballyline or on the hill in Shannon. All we needed was a bit of a reminder that this was the easy bit.

In ways, looking back on it, there's a certain element of guilt. I had played a game and a half of championship hurling for Clare and I had a Munster medal in my back pocket. The likes of Cyril Lyons had been toiling for over a decade. You're feeling guilty, in one sense, that you were so lucky and so privileged but you knew when you were talking to Cyril that you had his respect.

When I think back on the training we did that winter and spring, the group formed a bond around each other. We never lost sight of any of that when we started winning things.

Everything was in line for it to happen and it did happen, whereas the teams of the 70s and back further, they had great teams and great players. But they never got the rewards that we got. You'd be very thankful in that regard.

Even if we hadn't won the All-Ireland or Munster that year, I was having a ball being involved with the Clare team. That's all I ever wanted, to be playing with players I really looked up to; the likes of Jim McInerney, Cyril Lyons and Jamesie O'Connor.

The Laois game was a great start for me and I kept the jersey for a couple more games. Frank Lohan, Fergal Hegarty and myself had been brought into the panel.

Seánie McMahon was getting a run at centre-back, Anthony Daly was playing out on the wing and Brian Lohan was gone in full-back. Mike O'Halloran was also new to the set-up, as were Stephen McNamara and Conor Clancy. It was an exciting time for a young lad to be involved.

Everyone would have this perception, under Ger, Mike and Tony, that we were really intense, goal-driven and that nothing was going to get in our way. Nothing could be further from the truth. The best performances we ever gave were when we were relaxed.

We knew what we had to do, and we just went out and did it. There was no roaring or shouting or threats issued against anyone that they had to do this… or else it was going to be curtains.

There was a trust and understanding along the lines of… *We know the lads are training hard and the natural consequence of that is that they're going to play okay.* That mutual respect was there.

When I got a call to join the Clare panel in September or October of 1994, Mike Mac rang our house phone. He didn't talk to me though. He spoke to my mother. All he said was, 'Tell Ollie that we're training on Tuesday evening over in Ballyline and if he wants to be part of the panel, he'll be there'.

That was it. I was standing 10 feet from my mother but he didn't want to talk to me.

Even when I joined the gardaí, there were no mobile phones. It would have been in the winter of 1997. You got a phone call on a Friday evening to say that you were starting on the Monday. That's the way the world worked and that was everyone's house. There was no panic and there was no rushing.

You weren't getting a phone call asking, 'Where are you now?'

I had come on as a sub against Galway in the league in 1994 before Christmas. I was put in marking Pat Malone. I went in to challenge him for the first ball I went for. I bounced off him and my legs went from under me. As he was running off, his heel came back up and hit me under the chin and burst me. I never felt as low.

I'll never forget that moment and the complete embarrassment of being out on the field with a great player like Pat Malone. I felt that I didn't belong there at all. But it's how you dust yourself down and how you come out of that moment that tells a lot.

We were level going into injury time and I scored a point to put us ahead. It was the first time in a couple of decades that Clare would have won a game in Galway. I was fierce excited, thinking that I was going to get all of the headlines. There were three minutes of injury time played and Jim McInerney got 2-1. There wasn't a mention of Ollie Baker again.

I played a junior B hurling league final against Naoise Jordan. Noel Purcell, his godson, was playing in goals for us. Naoise was playing corner-forward for Parteen at the time. It was about 1991. I was 17. Naoise did everything in his power to score a goal. Noel didn't care if he let in 10 goals, as long as Naoise didn't get one.

I love being involved in clubs and hearing the stories of the junior B team. I played junior B and junior A hurling before I got a break to play intermediate for St Joseph's. Jim O'Donnell was on our team. He was a guard in Ennis and was on the Limerick 1973 panel. He hurt his leg before the '73 All-Ireland final. He would have been a great mentor for me. The ball just seemed to stick to him. He'd be everywhere the ball landed and you'd think he never moved at all.

He'd guide you through a game and tell you that you were taking too much out of the ball or going for a ball that there was no need to go for. Or if you're not going to get it, to sit back. This was exactly what a 16 or 17-year-old needed to hear… and you were hearing it from a legend.

Players aren't given the room to develop in club games now. If you don't make a development squad by the time you're 15, you can forget about ever playing for the county. Young lads aren't going to pick up how to play the game.

Junior hurling back then was a great learning ground.

I remember playing Scariff in one of my first years playing junior and a bit of a row started. My hurley was gone from my hand, although I hadn't dropped it to go fighting. A few lads were jumping in and I turned to face this lad who had a hurley.

He looked at me in amazement as if to say… *Where's your hurley? What kind of an ape are you?* He rose his hurley and I got out of there.

Jim O'Donnell told me after to never leave a hurley out of my hand again.

You bring those things with you and you wonder if young lads are getting that guidance nowadays. I don't think they are.

99

STEPHEN McNAMARA

CLARE 1-17 LIMERICK 0-11
Munster SHC Final
Semple Stadium, Thurles
JULY 9, 1995

Winning an All-Ireland title in his first summer with Clare was amazing for Stephen McNamara (above, tussling with Martin Hanamy of Offaly in the final), but claiming the Munster title against Limerick earlier that year was even more magical.

★ **CLARE:** D Fitzgerald (1-0); M O'Halloran, B Lohan, F Lohan; L Doyle, S McMahon (0-1), A Daly; F Hegarty (0-1), O Baker; F Tuohy (0-1), PJ O'Connell (0-4), J O'Connor (0-6); **S McNamara (0-1)**, C Clancy (0-2), G O'Loughlin (0-1). Subs: J McInerney for Tuohy, C Lyons for Clancy

★ **LIMERICK:** J Quaid; S McDonagh, M Nash, D Nash; D Clarke, C Carey, T Herbert; M Houlihan, S O'Neill; F Carroll (0-1), G Kirby (0-6), M Galligan (0-3); TJ Ryan, Pat Heffernan (0-1), D Quigley. Subs: T Hayes for Herbert, B Tobin for Carroll, D Barry for Hayes.

THE ACTION

SIXTY-THREE YEARS AFTER Clare had last won a Munster Hurling Championship, the emotional dam burst uncontrollably in Semple Stadium.

A year earlier, Limerick had beaten Clare by nine points in the Munster final and the Banner County seemed as far away as ever from achieving their dream of winning Munster. On this occasion, Clare got everything right. Everyone performed and no Clare man left anything in the dressing-room or on the training field.

A sign of Clare's mental and physical toughness was the fact that Seánie McMahon was fit to play, five weeks after breaking his collarbone against Cork in the Munster semi-final. McMahon had a big task on his hands, marking Gary Kirby, but the St Joseph's Doora-Barefield man was absolutely superb throughout the 70 minutes.

While the final scoreline looks comprehensive, for much of the first-half Limerick looked likely to hold onto their Munster crown. They led by three points after 22 minutes, having scored four successive points. However, Clare hit some crucial scores. Jamesie O'Connor pointed a free won by Ollie Baker, while Conor Clancy was fouled for a penalty. That came in the 28th minute, and Clare goalkeeper Davy Fitzgerald come up to take the penalty and he decisively dispatched it to the Limerick net.

Gary Kirby pointed twice for Limerick before O'Connor equalised, following a foul on Fergie Tuohy. The Clarecastle man then put over a superb point from play, just before the interval, to put Clare into a 1-5 to 0-7 interval lead. Clare were now backed by the breeze and, more importantly, they really believed that they were going to do it.

They outscored Limerick by 0-12 to 0-4 in that second-half. Their lung-bursting and character-forming training schedule, in Ballyline and the hill in Shannon, stood to them. The longer the game went on, the more Clare controlled it.

★★★★★

66

THE 1995 MUNSTER final was my first start for Clare.

That day, to me, was the greatest moment. I know the All-Ireland was special but with the hardship going back to 1955 in trying to win Munster… that meant that winning Munster in '95 was massive.

We weren't going down to play a match. We were going down to do a job.

That was the difference.

I got called into the senior panel after the 1994 under-21 Munster final against Waterford in Fermoy. The under-21 had gone well for me. We lost, but Loughnane called me up. But with the club season dragging on, I got my knee operated on in January of 1995. I had lost all interest in playing. I was enjoying life at 22.

In April of '95, Clare played Waterford in the semi-final of the league. I went down with Paudie O'Connell, his wife Orla and his brother Damien. We went down for the day out and we had a good few pints in Derek Browne's.

Mike Mac (McNamara) came in and said, 'Where have you been for the last three months? I've been looking for you'. This wouldn't happen now but he said to me, 'There's training tomorrow night!'

He had been very good to me at under-21, so when he said, 'You're coming back!'… I knew I had to. Mike Mac had a great relationship with my mother. He could ring her on a Monday and ask, 'How's your man getting on? He looks a bit tired.'

'Was he out… what's going on with him?'

He had a great relationship with the mothers, and he had them keeping us on our toes then.

They were different times. There were no phones and you didn't see anyone unless you were at training. There was no contact afterwards. That's the way it was.

After I got the call, we trained the following night at St Flannan's. Two weeks later, Clare played Kilkenny in the league final.

We were beaten and then we played Cork two or three weeks after that in the Munster semi-final in the Gaelic Grounds.

I came on at half-time… and I hit five glorious wides.

Loughnane said that he had never seen a Clare forward like me. 'Normally after one or two wides, they'd stop shooting… but you kept going. Is this a new thing?'

Then he started me in the final.

At that stage, we'd know the team on the Thursday or the Friday. It was in 1997 and '98 that the madness started.

That's where my 1995 came out of!

It was summer and things were speeding up.

Maybe I was lucky that I had missed the league. I wouldn't be the greatest man for the wet and muck.

I was sitting beside Fergie Tuohy on the bus. Fergie was like a father to me, trying to mind me. He was talking away all the way to Thurles. We used to have a puckaround in Cashel. I remember going into the match and you could see nothing but Limerick flags. I'd say it was five to one Limerick support-wise.

I ran onto a ball in the first couple of minutes, down the wing. I tapped it along and I thought it was gone over the line but there was about 10 yards in it. I realised then how big the pitch was.

Later on, I was running with the ball and trying to get past Ciarán Carey. I gave it to Conor Clancy. We got a penalty, but Fergie Tuohy bawled me out of it for not putting it over the bar. He was looking after me again!

It opened up in the second-half and we were able to throw it around a bit. I hit a ball over the bar from near the sideline and I'd say if I was in front of goal, I'd have probably missed it.

With about three or four minutes to go, Conor Clancy and myself ended up in around the square with the two Nash brothers, Declan and Mike. We were saying to each other, 'How are we going to cock this up?'… which would have been our tradition unfortunately down through the years.

The two boys said, 'Lads, ye're all right today. That's not going to happen!'

That was our first realisation that we were going to win and, in fairness to those boys and Stephen McDonagh, they came out to meet us on the Monday after the All-Ireland, when we came into Shannon Airport. Those three boys were waiting for us and we had a pint with them in the bar. That's the strength of the GAA.

That summer I was coming in, the sun was shining and the ball was hopping.

I was kind of lucky that I hadn't been exposed to the hammerings in 1993 and '94. Limerick didn't really know me and I didn't know what I was doing, which was one advantage.

I was too young to think about doubting myself. The doubts would have set in afterwards. In 1996 and '97, I'd be asking had I done this or that right? That's when the doubting started.

In 1995, I didn't know what I was doing.

It was all new and fresh. I had no league campaign or any senior experience before that. It was bold really by the lads, in a way. The massive advantage I had was pace. Fingers (PJ O'Connell) and Jamesie also had pace. Sparrow (Ger O'Loughlin) was as cute as the day was long, but I didn't see him with pace. Maybe he had it when he was younger!

When the final whistle blew, I had been the last person with the ball in front of the stand. The ref took it off me and I was met by Paul Nihill and Pajoe Keane from Éire Óg. There was a group of them on the hill... the year before, I was on the hill with them.

There was a bunch of them in it... David Pyne, Barry Keating, Tadghie Lyne and Deccie Tobin. They were my group.

The year before, we had been out all night the night before and then we went down to the Munster final. Twelve months later... *I'm playing*. It was a bit surreal.

I was young but I knew that this was big.

I was at the Munster finals in 1977, '78, '81 and '86 in Killarney... and 1993 and '94. We'd have known the hardship of Clare hurling all our lives. I wasn't immune to that. I grew up following Kerry and the Clare hurlers.

Even though my grandfather played for Limerick, Clare was our hurling team. That was it. My father is from the town. His uncle Joker Coote was on the 1914 All-Ireland-winning Clare team. It's there on both sides.

We had a bit to eat in the Anner Hotel and then Ger loaded up the bus.

I'll never forget the journey back to Ennis. It was the best bus journey I was ever on. I think it kind of told us all what it was really about.

When you see Brian Lohan and Ger Loughnane singing, you know there's something special going on. The bus was mayhem. Brilliant.

You were just mad for Galway in the All-Ireland semi-final after that.

Training-wise, I missed all the grind in late-1994 and early '95. The boys used to slag me about that, every now and again. Of course, I had to do it in 1996 and '97.

But remember, I had John Maughan in 1993 and '94. I had two years of Maughan when he was over the Clare footballers. Enough said. That opened my eyes… it was an education.

We were going out to Crusheen and we never saw a football. We were playing league games on a Sunday and we still hadn't seen a football. It gave me a grounding. Donie Buckley was involved then as well. You knew the kind of fitness levels you had to get up to. The boys won Munster in 1992 and I was brought in in '93.

1992 drove on the hurling an awful lot. You'd want to have been immune not to have felt the shakes against Dublin in the All-Ireland semi-final, when the footballers came out at the Canal End. I'll never forget the footballers for that. We saw how hard they were training and we knew that we had to train as hard.

Running out in Croke Park, against Galway in the 1995 All-Ireland semi-final, was the same thing. It couldn't but lift you.

I was fortunate enough in that as a dual player with Éire Óg, on a Saturday you could be playing in Newmarket, the 'Bridge or Kilkishen. Then the following Saturday, you'd be going to Kilkee, Doonbeg, Miltown or Liscannor.

I first saw Éire Óg in a county final in 1980.

When you look at the club you think of families like the Loftus', the Blakes, the Ryans, the Russells… and Smythie, Bombs McCarthy… all the boys I saw growing up.

When you go up to Croke Park and you're representing all of them, you couldn't but be proud. It's great what Shane O'Donnell has done after. We're ticking along as a club. We have players on the county football and hurling teams. That's what a GAA club in Ennis should be doing. We should be providing players and if we're not, we're not doing our job.

I'm from the town of Ennis and even outside of Éire Óg, to represent the town would mean as much. We had a shop on the Mill Road, where my father came out of. The McNamaras and the Cootes were strong town names. Outside of the Powers, on my mother's side in Kerry, we've a strong tradition. I'd be very proud of being from Ennis.

Éire Óg is one thing and Ennis is another. I'm a proud townie.

We won the Senior Football Championship with Faughs in 1994. Winning the championship with Faughs was a big thing. You're 21 and the main forward on the team. You were used to getting the belts and the hits.

I played under-21 hurling and football, junior hurling and football for Clare, as well as for Éire Óg and Faughs, which was an amalgamation of us and Doora-Barefield. I played on 11 or 12 teams in 1994.

There isn't a village, or some would say a pub, in the county that I don't know. That was the great thing about being a dual player for me.

If I hadn't been involved in the GAA, there's thousands of Clare people that I'd have never met. It's still nice to go to different parts of the county, go in somewhere and hold a conversation about that time or about the GAA.

All the boys would feel the same.

If I was back in Miltown, I'd call into Martin Flynn or any of the places around. You'd never have a problem going in anywhere because the one thing we all have in common is GAA. When I moved to Dublin, I was very fortunate to get involved with a couple of clubs. And go to Australia or the U.S.… and the GAA opens the door there too.

People don't realise the strength of the GAA. First of all, it's a fabulous game and it brings communities together. It's the politics that irritates me, but as regards growing up and making friends, the GAA is great.

We lose more than we win but that feeling you get from being in a dressing-room stays with you.

Everyone in their career has lost more games than they have won. It's great when you're winning but your friendships come out of when you're losing.

You still hang around with those people. You have so much in common with them.

When I look around my circle, there are still GAA people in it. You can't get away from them! If I tried, I couldn't and nor would I want to.

99

FRANK LOHAN
(& FERGIE TUOHY)

CLARE 1-13 OFFALY 2-8
All-Ireland SHC Final
Croke Park
SEPTEMBER 3, 1995

Frank Lohan had to hit the ground running in his first year with the Clare seniors in 1995, when he also got to play in the same line as his brother Brian for the first time (above, Brian and Frank team up against Johnny Dooley in the All-Ireland final).

★ **CLARE:** D Fitzgerald; M O'Halloran, B Lohan, **F Lohan**; L Doyle, S McMahon (O-3), A Daly (O-1); O Baker (O-1), J O'Connor (O-2); **F Tuohy (O-4)**, PJ O'Connell, F Hegarty (O-1); S McNamara, C Clancy, G O'Loughlin (O-1). Subs: E Taaffe (1-O) for McNamara, C Lyons for Clancy, A Neville for Taaffe.

★ **OFFALY:** D Hughes; S McGuckin, K Kinihan, M Hanamy; B Whelehan, H Rigney, K Martin; J Pilkington (1-O), D Regan (O-1); Johnny Dooley (O-5), John Troy (O-1), Joe Dooley; Billy Dooley (O-1), Pat O'Connor, M Duignan (1-O). Subs: D Pilkington for O'Connor, B Kelly for Joe Dooley.

THE ACTION

EVERY CLARE PERSON who was in Croke Park to witness Anthony Daly lift the Liam MacCarthy Cup in 1995 will never forget that moment. Of the many iconic moments from that day, Eamon Taaffe's goal, five minutes from time, is when every Clare supporter at the game or watching on television started to believe that it was going to happen. An Anthony Daly free from distance hit David Hughes' crossbar and bounced back into play. Taaffe connected with the loose ball to ram home the most iconic goal in the history of Clare hurling.

His immediate reward for finding the net? The Tubber man was instantly replaced by Clarecastle's Alan Neville.

What is often forgotten is that Johnny Dooley put over an equalising 50-metre free for the reigning All-Ireland champions a minute after Taaffe's goal. Clare managed to retain their composure though and Daly nailed a '65', while Jamesie O'Connor pointed the final score of the final to secure a two-point lead with just seconds left.

Unbelievably, Clare had done it and 81 years after they won their first All-Ireland, the county had its hands on the Liam MacCarthy Cup.

Another moment that stood out from that historic day was when a very driven-looking Ger Loughnane assured RTÉ's Marty Morrissey, and indeed the nation, that Clare were on their way.

'We're going to do it!' Loughnane said in a short half-time sideline interview, seconds before the game restarted.

Offaly had led 1-6 to 0-7 at half-time. Crucially, Fergal Hegarty and Ger O'Loughlin pointed before the half ended, ensuring that the deficit was more manageable. Sixteen minutes from time, Johnny Pilkington hit Offaly's second goal and it looked as if they might go on to retain their title. However, an inspired Fergie Tuohy, who hit four points from play, was central to keeping Clare in touch, until Taaffe struck for that era-defining goal.

★★★★★

66

THERE WAS PROBABLY a small bit of pressure on myself and Holly (Michael O'Halloran) going into the All-Ireland final.

We hadn't been brilliant in any of the matches and I certainly felt that I had a very dodgy 10 or 15 minutes in the semi-final against Galway. The team was very comfortable overall but I wouldn't have been happy with how my own game went in the semi-final.

But as a full-back line, we knew each other very well. Brian had been hurling brilliantly for a few years but myself and Mike were new to it.

I think everyone knew their job. Fitzy was a great goalie and we knew our roles in the full-back line. If we could make sure that the shots were taken from a certain distance out, we were confident that they'd be saved. Brian was very good at what he did and he brought huge presence to it.

Myself and Mike used to try and get the ball out to someone else to clear it, whether that was Dalo outside us or Brian inside… Seánie or Liam Doyle. There was as sweet a bunch of hurlers in the half-back line as you'd ever see. We were all very clear on our roles.

We felt that we were doing okay in the final but we let Offaly back into it with the goals. They weren't brilliant goals by Offaly by any means.

Brian's leg had started to come against him in the Galway game and that happened again in the final. I'd say his hamstring was gone. Coming into the game he was grand, but it went in the second-half. He was able to manage it and get through it. We got stronger as it went on and we got that bit of luck.

I had Billy Dooley that day. He was a brilliant hurler and I knew that I had my hands full. His brothers Joe and Johnny had a much higher profile, but that year and the year before, Billy was playing really great hurling. Offaly had very skilful players, who could do anything with the ball; the likes of John Troy and the Dooleys.

The reason I picked this game is because it was such a huge game for everyone but it was the one game that I just felt brilliant. I don't know how that will come across, but we felt powerful, even towards the end and we believed that we were going to see it out. It's a game that resonates with most Clare people. It was a highlight for an awful lot of people and I'm no different.

We got a break with Eamon's goal… coming back off the crossbar and then he finished it like he did. We were feeling very good as a collective and we were very fit. We always felt that we were going to finish stronger than most teams.

I was 20 and still living at home. Before a game, we'd go for a few pucks on the Saturday, particularly early in the year. On All-Ireland final day, I think my dad dropped us down to the Oakwood Hotel in Shannon. We flew to Dublin and had the breakfast. Then we'd go for a sleep for an hour or two.

I remember Seán Hehir came into the dressing-room. I think he was commentating for Radió na Gaeltachta. He was absolutely hyped. We seemed to be much calmer. He was absolutely bursting and hoping for a great day.

We were in the old dressing-rooms beside the canal. Micheál Ó Muircheataigh also came in. I don't remember being hugely overcome by nerves. I just felt that we were ready to have a go.

We were very confident that we had the work done. Any team that gets to an All-Ireland final has the work done. It's taken as a given but it does give you great confidence. The management team would have been re-enforcing that. We knew what to expect. It was all very planned.

We had our warm-up at the Aer Rianta centre in Dublin. We felt very good.

It was so new to me, with it being my first year. The Munster final was when I started thinking… *This is really serious stuff.*

Munster was so important to Ger and the whole team but then the All-Ireland brought it to a different level altogether. I don't think you had to be on the team to see how that was the case. The entire county, home and abroad, felt it.

I was called into the panel in September of 1994.

I was driving my dad's car and I met Ger in the car park in Shannon Town Centre. I was going in and Ger was going in the opposite direction. He said, 'You'll come in on Tuesday?'

That was it. I remember Brian saying to me that Ger and Len Gaynor had thought about bringing me in during the summer of 1994 but they didn't.

We were in Crusheen and we were just starting back. I used to travel up and down with Ger from Shannon to training. Brian was in London that winter. Ger was the school principal at St Aidan's and had lived in Shannon for a long time.

I was very lucky in that I got a full league behind me before the championship. We got to the league final, so I got to play in a good number of matches. The All-Ireland final was then my fourth game in the championship. I didn't start against Cork, but I started the Munster final and then Galway in the semi-final.

I played for Clare a good number of years. I won things in the first three years but that was it... I didn't win anything again with the county. We would have tried unbelievably hard to get over the line but we didn't, so I feel extremely lucky to be involved in those early years.

We had a brilliant management team and a great bunch of teammates.

A good number of the lads, who were the backbone of the team, had painful defeats behind them, although they weren't much older than the rest of us. We got on a roll that year and things went for us. Ger was very driven and knew what he wanted.

I didn't have huge ambition hurling-wise when I was growing up. Although, in saying that, I did want to play minor for Clare. I loved sport and I still do. Growing up in Shannon, sport was very important and at underage we won a lot.

We had a lot of great players, great coaches... and a growing population.

Once I went down to UCC to college, I loved my first year there playing freshers and I made the Fitzgibbon team. I was playing with brilliant inter-county players. Pat Hartnett from Cork had come back to college. We played a lot of the senior clubs in Cork and I was able to hold my own. You'd start thinking that maybe these other counties aren't miles ahead of us.

My progress was incremental in that I played Clare minor. Then in 1994 we had a very good Clare under-21 team. It wouldn't be a team that would be talked about all that much but we probably let a final slip away against Waterford.

Up to 1995, I wouldn't have played all that much with Brian.

He was three years older than me and I wouldn't have been making his underage teams. The teams in Wolfe Tones were very competitive. Brian's minor team won the championship and they were very, *very* good. They had the likes of Jack Keary, Paul Lee, Paul O'Rourke and Seán Power. They were great players for Wolfe Tones.

I played one or two junior matches for Wolfe Tones, when I was starting to play adult hurling. I played wing-back a bit and also wing-forward. I don't think I ever played in the full-back line with Brian for the club.

I was always a bit out the field… either wing-back or centre-back.

There are many facets to Shannon. It was a great place to live and a great place to grow up. My parents are still there and I have an office there as well. Not to over-egg the importance of sport but the 80s and 90s were a very important time for the club and the community. We were only a new town at that time, and a new town can have a strange dynamic.

Wolfe Tones is very proud of the contribution it has made to the town and to the county. We're all blow-ins to the town in some ways, although I grew up in Shannon. I didn't live anywhere else but Shannon. I've seen other places… and your family could be there three or four generations, but they are still considered *blow-ins*. There can be negative connotations in some places and it holds back some communities. But not ours! The day after the 1995 final, we flew back into Shannon and there was a big crowd there. My grandmother came up on the roof and she was a pretty good age at the time.

The players I played with, their parents would have been from different parts of the county or the country. We're a dual club and we were very proud to contribute to 1995. And, after that, the following year was a great year for our club. We won our first senior championship in 1996, something I'll never forget.

A lot of people in the county would know my dad Gus.

He loved sport and played for loads of different teams. He was a guard based in Shannon and that's how we ended up there. He was a brilliant support to us, but he wouldn't get too excited or too down.

We put an awful lot into it and he would be down if things did go against us but if it went well, he'd be delighted.

But, if it didn't go well, he'd still buy the papers and read them.

He wouldn't be trying to give us advice. I've a few young boys and maybe I could take a leaf from his book. Dad was very measured in his outlook. Himself and our mother would have had great times going to matches. Our mum would have got quite excited at games, hoping that things went okay for us.

The days after the final were a whirlwind. They were great times, never to be forgotten. I think we were in Brogan's in Ennis on the Monday night, Tuesday morning. Everyone has their own memories of those days.

We were so lucky to have brilliant people over us.

I obviously meet Brian but I wouldn't meet too many of the others.

I'm living in Galway now and we try to meet once a year. I look forward to meeting the lads, they're a great bunch. It was a super time for hurling but it was much bigger than that too, for ourselves and for the county.

It was a privilege to be part of it.

99

FERGIE TUOHY

Even though he starred with four points against Offaly in the All-Ireland final in 1995, Fergie Tuohy (above, second from right in the front row in the team photo before the game) believes his best game that summer was in the Munster final victory over Tipperary.

THINGS DIDN'T GET off to the best of starts that morning. I was the only one left in the house in Clarecastle. Everyone else was gone to Dublin.

I got up and said I'd have a quick shower. I hopped in and the next thing there was a huge flash and a spark from the box in the shower. I jumped out straight away.

That was the end of the shower.

I knew that my mother's sister was coming to mind the house while everyone was away. So I wrote a note and left it on the kitchen table.

Shower faulty. Do not use.

Gone to Dublin to win the All-Ireland for Clare.

I said I'd throw that in.

We were flying up. We met at the Oakwood Hotel in Shannon to be brought to the runway. Sparrow picked us up and drove us down to Shannon… and we got on the bus.

Jim McInerney tells this story…

We were driving onto the runway, which was about 10 '65s' away. But there was a barrier in the way and the driver was going to reverse.

The next thing, McInerney and Loughnane got out.

They lifted the barrier off the hinges. I took no notice, but Jim took it as a sign of defiance and that we weren't going to take any step back that day.

There was going to be no more reversing.

We went to the Trust House Forte Hotel in Dublin and had our breakfast.

We had gone up like that for the semi-final too. Before the semi-final, I was having breakfast and I said to Jamesie that I was tired.

He said he was tired too. Jamesie said it to Loughnane.

Ten minutes later, we were given a key and two of us were put into a room… myself and Jamesie were sharing.

Jamesie pulled the curtains, and I opened a window.

Jamesie was asking, what was I doing?

I was having a fag.

'Ah, no!' Jamesie was saying. He couldn't believe it.

It wasn't as if I was a chain smoker… it was to calm the nerves. The next time that happened was for the final and I wasn't sharing with Jamesie. I think it was Hego (Fergal Hegarty).

Before the final, we lay down to rest and the Formula One racing was on TV. I had no interest but you'd have to watch it anyway. You'd be hoping that the build-up for the minor final would be on, but we'd only get 10 minutes of it anyway.

Loughnane said that in the week leading up to the final, that we would have doubts.

Were we fit enough?

Have we enough training done?

Loughnane said that this would come to everybody at some stage but that it wouldn't come to us at the same time. You could be sitting at home, or on the bus or just about to take to the field… everyone has those doubts creeping in at some stage.

I remember being on the bus going down Jones' Road. I started to question myself, but then I remembered that Loughnane had already given us the answer. And the answer was that we were ready.

When we got near Croke Park, it was some experience. You didn't know whether to look at the crowd or pull the curtain.

We had played National Leagues there but we had never been there when there was a full house. The week before, we had gone up training. We did a few hurling drills and Loughnane was saying… 'It's made for you. This is your stage!'

When Loughnane *got* you, you were meant to be already fit.

You were able to tolerate anything he was throwing at you then. If you weren't fit, you wouldn't be able to put up with the way things were directed at you and the push that was coming from them. When you were physically fit, it helped with your mental fitness. You *were* ready.

If you start thinking too much about the game, you mightn't puck a ball. Just before we were going out, next thing Cyril (Lyons) brought us into the shower area. He had a ball in his hands.

'If you don't have the ball, you cannot influence the game!' he reminded us.

For me, that simplified it and brought it back down to basics. You've got to get possession.

I was wing-forward on Kevin Martin.

He made one or two darts in the first-half and struck the ball wide. I got a point in the half and I met Daithí Regan over by the Cusack Stand with a shoulder, which the referee deemed was a foul. I thought I was doing alright but at the start of the second-half, I found myself in corner-forward.

I don't remember getting instructions to go out the field, but I drifted out anyway and got on one or two balls… and hit them over the bar.

When it was coming down the stretch, we were playing into the Canal End. Offaly were after getting the Johnny Pilkington goal.

They were pressing and pressing again.

The ball was bobbling around the edge of the square, but I couldn't see what was happening. For a minute, I looked up at the big screen … to see what was happening. I found it really unusual to do that but it was so crowded back there, I couldn't see.

The next thing, I saw Frank coming out with the ball on the screen!

People might say that I played well in the 1995 final, and any day you win an All-Ireland medal and put over four points, is one that will live with you forever. But I thought the Munster final was my best game in a Clare jersey. I hit five points.

I thought I was on my game. I was on Turlough Herbert. Limerick took him off at half-time. They brought on Tadhg Hayes, and took him off. That was when you could only make three substitutions. In the first couple of minutes, I met Mike Nash on the sideline. He was coming up the line by the '21'…. I dosed him and I was sickened myself, but I had to get up straight away.

I also thought I did reasonably well in the 1997 Munster final on Colm Bonnar. I met him in The Burlington Hotel after the All-Ireland that year. I had been taken off in that game. He told me that because of the Munster final, he had been waiting for me to come in centre-forward on him. But I was started in the corner.

I had got injured after the Munster final running for a ball with Jamesie, and I was out for the 1997 All-Ireland semi-final against Kilkenny.

I did a fitness test that morning. I was sprinting grand but I wasn't turning, although I was saying I was all right. Mike Mac shook his head though and Gilly came in.

I was delighted that I was named for the final.

I was on Paul Shelly in that game. One ball came in and I let it out over the line. After 20 minutes, I was taken off. Loughnane brought Hego on, and put him on the wing. But I felt I could have been given a run on the wing.

Before 1995, you'd always be doubting yourself and wondering were you good enough… or would you freeze? We got momentum as the year went on, but by 1997 the team was established. We had been caught in 1996 and that left a great desire in the team.

But I don't think we would have won three in-a-row if we had won in 1996.

What we found in ourselves in order to beat Tipp came from a place that we had never been before. We had never gone that deep into ourselves. We were all playing hurling for the love of it and the fun, but we had to go and find something more.

On the day of the 1997 Munster final, we went down to Cork early.

We were staying in the Hayfield Manor. We had a bit of breakfast. I was rooming with PJ O'Connell. We were smoking a few fags away and a knock came to the door. We thought it was Loughnane.

There was a cloud of smoke... but it was Baker looking for a fag as well.

Then... another knock came to the door, and it was young Barry Loughnane and Conor McNamara giving us our jerseys. We hadn't played many games in Páirc Uí Chaoimh. We knew that the dressing-rooms were tight, so Loughnane said he'd give us our jerseys and we'd go into the stadium in our tracksuits.

We came in by the Blackrock end.

We were up on top of the hill and we were going to descend down behind the dressing-rooms. The Tipperary bus was already there. We could see them.

They were about 200 yards away but Mal, our driver, didn't want to pull up behind them and wait on them. He didn't want us *waiting* on them.

We'd have been second in line straight away.

Later, as we were coming out of the tunnel, there was a railing in front of us. The bench for the team photo was about 10 yards in. To a man, everyone jumped over the railing. We weren't side-stepping anything... we were going straight through.

Everyone was on the same page that day.

We started with a blast.

Myself, PJ and Jamesie were in the half-forward line. I was wearing 10. I thought I'd be on Ramie Ryan or Conal Bonnar.

Loughnane told us to, 'Stick together for Amhrán na bhFiann and... when it's over... Fergie, you go in centre-forward!' I went in centre-forward on Colm Bonnar. The very first ball, I was about two yards in front of him. I pulled at fresh air. Then I realised that I'd had loads of time. I had to compose myself. You think because the adrenaline is going, that you have to go at 100 miles an hour.

I got the next ball, jinked him and I was up and running. I played reasonably well.

We went 10 points up.

They had a cross-field ball… Colin Lynch intercepted it and drove it over. But they fought back and Leahy had a great chance to win it at the end.

For Clarecastle, in the 1994 club semi-final against the 'Bridge, I scored seven points. I was wing-forward. Victor O'Loughlin was centre-forward.

With about five minutes to go, he roared… 'GOALS… GOALS!!'

But I was roaring… 'POINTS… POINTS!'

The next thing, I got four in-a-row in about six or seven minutes. That was Jamesie territory, not mine! We got out of it with a draw and won the replay.

We won the championship.

That kind of put me into Ger Loughnane's thinking for 1995.

Our club is our DNA. In the early 80s, Clarecastle won a Clare Cup. I was 15 or 16 going up watching them. The goal at 15 was to be playing senior. It was mapped out for me in my own mind. That's what I wanted. I wasn't thinking of inter-county.

We won two minors in 1986 and '87. I played junior B and intermediate too, and played in an intermediate final in 1987. In '88, I was brought into the senior panel and straight into the team.

It was all about the club for us at the time. We were lucky enough that we had seasoned men in Clarecastle… they kept us focused; we listened to them.

It was similar with Clare. We had men on the management team and on the field who had that edge.

They loved their hurling and they enjoyed it, but they were winners.

99

GERRY McINERNEY

SIXMILEBRIDGE 5-10 DUNLOY 2-6
All-Ireland Club SHC Final
Croke Park
MARCH 17, 1996

Five years after ending his Clare career, Gerry McInerney had the honour of leading Sixmilebridge out onto Croke Park where they became the first Clare team to capture the All-Ireland title. Gerry (inset) got to lead his teammates again (above) when they were honoured 25 years later.

★ **SIXMILEBRIDGE:** D Fitzgerald; M O'Halloran, K McInerney, M Twomey; C Chaplin, J O'Connell, P Hayes; J Chaplin (O-3), N Earley; David Chaplin (2-1), F Quilligan, M Conlon; D McInerney (1-O), Danny Chaplin (1-O), **G McInerney (1-3)**. Subs: N O'Gorman for Hayes, N Gilligan (O-3) for Quilligan, I Mulready for Danny Chaplin.

★ **DUNLOY:** S Elliot; N McCamphill, P Molloy, S McIlhatton; S McMullan (O-2), G O'Kane, S Mullan; F McMullan (O-1), C McGuckian; N Elliot; T McGrath (1-1), J Elliot; E McKee, G O'Kane (O-1), A Elliot (1-1). Subs: B Gunning for McCamphill, M Molloy for J Elliot, L Richmond for McMullan.

THE ACTION

SIXMILEBRIDGE HEADED FOR Dublin on the morning of their All-Ireland club final meeting with Dunloy as warm favourites.

The Clare and Munster champions had struggled to emerge from their own county, but once they did, they seemed to hurl with freedom and ambition. They knew that they had a panel of players capable of bringing the All-Ireland club title back to Clare for the first time.

They just had to prove it and that's exactly what transpired.

Their 13-point win, though, was somewhat flattering and didn't do justice to Dunloy, who had competed superbly against Birr when they met in the 1995 All-Ireland club final. The Offaly and Leinster champions needed a second chance to get the better of their opponents from Antrim, after they drew 0-9 apiece on March 17, 1995.

Suitably forewarned, Sixmilebridge made a superb start when Danny Chaplin netted the first of Sixmilebridge's goals after just 50 seconds. To underline their tenacity, Dunloy hit back with four successive points. In fact, Sixmilebridge didn't add to their tally for 18 minutes.

They struck for their second goal in the 20th minute, when David Chaplin put away the first of his two goals on the big stage. Minutes later, Sixmilebridge raised their third green flag of the half. A Noel Earley delivery found Danny Chaplin and the full-forward placed Gerry McInerney, who buried it.

Now 3-1 to 0-4 ahead, Sixmilebridge were on their way. Further points from David Chaplin and McInerney helped them into a 3-4 to 1-4 interval lead. Dunloy threw everything at their opponents in the early minutes of the second-half but Davy Fitzgerald denied them. However, Alastair Elliot did breach the Sixmilebridge defence five minutes into the second-half and put away his side's first goal.

Fifteen minutes from time, Sixmilebridge led 3-5 to 2-6 and the game was in the balance.

However, two additional goals from David Chaplin and Declan McInerney put Sixmilebridge on the road to glory. There was no way back now for Dunloy. While Sixmilebridge's attackers were lauded for their goal-scoring prowess, John O'Connell, Kevin McInerney and Michael O'Halloran were superb in defence.

★ ★ ★ ★ ★

"

MICHAEL MCDONAGH IS a local racehorse trainer and he had gallops at the back of my house. He had a sand gallop and a grass gallop. They were both a mile of a circuit.

In the 'Bridge they would always say that I wouldn't kill myself at training. I'd do enough to get by but I'd have to say that year, I put in a phenomenal effort.

I felt that at my age, I had to do an awful lot more than just normal club training sessions so that I wouldn't be made a show of. I used to go in there several nights a week. One night I'd do six laps of the grass gallop. The next night I'd do the sand gallop. It was the first time that I really did an awful lot of training away from the designated club nights.

I never trained as hard. I felt that I had to do more. Funnily enough, when we started getting the results, it became easier to face into the gallops and put in the work.

I walked away from the Clare senior team in 1991.

I was only 29 and probably would have had a few more years had I stayed at it. So when the opportunity came in 1996, I knew that the sun was setting on my career and that opportunities were going to be few and far between after that.

In 1995 we were very poor in a lot of our games in the championship. It was daylight robbery that we won the county final against Scariff. David Chaplin got a goal in the last minute. I thought there were a few minutes of time left. We were two points down and I took a shot for a point, thinking that we had time.

But the ball hit the upright and came back into play. Davy Chaplin finished the rebound. We robbed it from Scariff but after that, we were a team transformed.

We went to Ballygunner and scored five goals in Walsh Park against them. Then we beat Nenagh in the final, which I think was our most accomplished performance that year. Everything went for us and I thought we played exceptional hurling that day. In the All-Ireland semi-final, we played Sarsfields, who were the yardstick. They had won four All-Ireland club titles in the decade before that. We beat them, scoring another five goals.

We played Dunloy in the All-Ireland final and scored five goals again.

It has always been part of the history of the 'Bridge that we always play better hurling once we get out of the county. The pressure locally is always to win your championship and when you win that, you can throw off the shackles.

That year, nobody came within nine points of us in Munster or in the All-Ireland series, and in four of those games we scored five goals. That, to me, was saying that we were creating chances and we were clinical in our scoring. If you're scoring five goals, you'd have to be awful porous in defence not to win a match.

You're going to score 10 or 12 points with your five goals and that's putting you up close to the 30-point mark.

I ended up the top scorer in the Clare championship, and I scored 5-18 in the Munster and All-Ireland campaigns. Maybe the hard work in the horse gallops paid off!

We beat Patrickswell in the Munster club final in 1984. It was played on December 16, and then we decided to take a break. When we came back in January, we felt we had slipped. So in 1995 we made a decision, after winning the Munster club against Nenagh, that we'd take a week off and then go back to it.

So we actually trained throughout the Christmas to keep fellas tuned in and not let the guard down, where they might cut loose.

I remember one night at the end of January, the place was covered in snow. We used to run a mile of a loop around the village, which was lit up. Every time we passed the GAA field, the management team were there with a load of snowballs and the stragglers were pelted with them.

We had gone down to training expecting it to be cancelled but Jim Fawl said… 'NO!!'

I'd say he was testing fellas' mental resolve as well.

Jim was the manager, Pat Morey the coach and we had Mick O'Shea and John Nihill as the selectors. In fairness, they were very professional in their approach. No player wanted for anything.

For the All-Ireland club final, we replicated what the Clare hurlers did in 1995 in terms of their travel arrangements. We flew from Shannon to Dublin, went to the hotel, had a sleep and then went for a puckaround.

Ian Mulready was captain but he broke his hand. He wasn't fit to start, although he took off the plaster for the final and he was named as a sub. I was the vice-captain, so I led the team out and around behind the Artane Boys Band, as it was called then. But we brought on Ian, late in the game, and he accepted the cup.

You can burn up an awful lot of energy getting hyped up before a game. The forwards would go into a group and talk among ourselves. The boys in defence would do the same. There was no roaring or shouting. It was all very controlled and very calm from the players. If you get too wound up, you can leave a lot in the dressing-room.

We left the roaring and shouting to Jim, who was very much a fire and brimstone man. The big thing the players drummed into one another was… *This is the opportunity… and are we going to live the rest of our lives with regrets?* We knew we were good enough. We knew that if we went out and performed like we knew we could, we were going to be the first Clare club to win the All-Ireland title.

Jim would be excitable, but he'd put the hair standing on the back of your neck as you were going out.

We were on first that day. The club provided transport for the wives and girlfriends but they got caught in the St Patrick's Day parade in Dublin. When they got to Croke Park, the match was on and they had missed Danny Chaplin's goal. That was the only downside.

People were saying beforehand that because Dunloy were a team from the North, we should be able to beat them. But the previous year, they had played Birr and were beaten in a replay. They should have beaten Birr the first day. People didn't give them credit for how good a team they were.

In the final, with 15 minutes to go, there was only a point or two in it. We got a couple of rapid-fire goals and once we got them, that was it. But up until then, it was very much in the melting pot. They had quite a number of the Antrim team, people like Gregory O'Kane, Alistair Elliot and Gary O'Kane. They were hurlers that would get on any team.

I did alright. I think I scored 1-4 or 1-5. It was a workmanlike performance but we hit five goals and that showed the potential we had in attack. I felt we delivered in spades that year.

Danny Chaplin was the target man at full-forward… and Danny was a great man to get possession. It was funnelled at him and we fed off the breaking ball, off him.

In the last number of years, the 'Bridge has developed substantially and you have an awful lot of people coming in making Sixmilebridge their home. Even that time, you had flags up in houses where I didn't know who the people were. They weren't native to the 'Bridge but everyone bought into the buzz that was in the parish. It gave them a sense of identity I suppose or pride in the place that they were in now. It was their new club.

Even that day, there were people out on Croke Park with 'Bridge colours that weren't from Sixmilebridge but they had come to live here and wanted to integrate into the community. There's no better organisation to give a community identity than the GAA.

We stayed in The Burlington Hotel that night. The following day, we came home by train and there was a massive homecoming in the Square.

The first people I met when we got off the bus were a couple from Wexford, Brendan and Breda Flood. I had been secretary of the 'Bridge minor club in 1984. We went to Féile in Wexford and our host club was Oulart the Ballagh, the home of Mick Jacob. I stayed in Brendan and Breda's house. They were my host family.

They had been at the match and had driven all the way to the 'Bridge for the homecoming. Things like that stand out.

I remember getting off the stage after the presentation... seeing the late Johnny Frost and Jimmy Corry crying. They had done so much for the 'Bridge club over the years. Johnny played and Jimmy had been an administrator and a selector. It was similar to Clare in 1995. People involved in the club didn't think they'd have seen this day either.

Then, the following day, the club sponsor took the panel to Spain for a week. Away we went for a week thanks to Dominic Murphy (RIP). The only downside to that was while we had a ball, maybe a few more days at home would have been ideal. It was only the one night in the 'Bridge and then we were gone.

When we came back, things had died down a bit. Maybe we should have stayed around for a few days to celebrate with the locals first, before we went on the holiday but that wasn't the way it was organised.

We were also very fortunate in that Dominic of Shannon Precision Engineering was an extremely generous sponsor and Trixie Toomey (RIP) rowed in as well with financial support.

The last thing you wanted was to have regrets. We felt that we had a team good enough to win an All-Ireland club title. We wanted to seize the moment and the players bought into that. We knew that we might never again find ourselves in that position. *Were we going to regret it for the rest of our lives?* That was always the mentality.

We trained early mornings and in the evenings. There was always food provided for us.

There was no expense spared but everyone saw the bigger picture. It wasn't all handouts that we got either. Players fundraised as well and the club rowed in behind us. There was a great unity of purpose. We all knew that winning the All-Ireland club was achievable.

We won the Clare Championship in 1992 and '93.

Clarecastle won it in 1994... and we won it in '95.

Yet at Clare training sessions, apparently Ger Loughnane used to always refer to Clarecastle as potential All-Ireland club champions. Here we were after being beaten in two Munster club finals and then winning one, yet we weren't being considered as potential All-Ireland club champions. That was one line that came out a few times in training.

We got to the Munster club final in 1992. I thought we were unlucky not to have beaten Kilmallock. We had the winning of the game but we just didn't see it out. We were undone by the scoring prowess of Paddy Kelly, who was a Limerick hurler... I think he got 2-7 out of 2-12.

We were beaten by three points, having been in a commanding position. The following year, we got back to the Munster club final against Toomevara. That was the one where Seán Stack was playing with us and he was also coaching Toomevara. That day, we just didn't perform. If you give a performance and you're beaten, well and good but if you don't perform, you've an awful lot of misgivings.

We knew we had a team that was capable of going further but it was just about getting it right.

1979 was also a year that was very significant for me. I played in the minor, under-21 and senior finals that year with the 'Bridge.

We won all three and, as far as I know, I'm the only club hurler to have done that. I also captained St Flannan's that year to win the Dr Harty Cup and the All-Ireland colleges. It was the first all-Clare Harty Cup winning team.

My highest score of the three games was in the senior final. I scored 2-2. We beat St Brendan's in the final, which was an amalgamation of Kilmaley and Doora-Barefield.

After winning the All-Ireland club in 1996, the following year we were beaten by Wolfe Tones. And we were beaten by Doora-Barefield in the last game I played for the club. They got a last-minute goal in the 1997 county semi-final.

I ended up in hospital.

I was put there by my own man. My own player ran into me when we were going for a ball. I ended up concussed and I had to get a few stitches in my lip.

That was a lovely way to sign out!

FERGAL HEGARTY

LIMERICK 1-13 CLARE 0-15
Munster SHC Semi-Final
Gaelic Grounds, Limerick
JUNE 16, 1996

Fergal Hegarty (above, beating Liam Sheedy in the 1997 All-Ireland final) believes the loss to Limerick the year before was the most dramatic day of his hurling career.

★ **CLARE:** D Fitzgerald; M O'Halloran, B Lohan, F Lohan; L Doyle, S McMahon (0-3), A Daly; O Baker, **F Hegarty**; F Tuohy (0-3), PJ O'Connell, J O'Connor (0-5); S McNamara, C Clancy, G O'Loughlin (0-2). Subs: E Taaffe (0-2) for Clancy, R O'Hara for O'Connell, C Lyons for McNamara.

★ **LIMERICK:** J Quaid; S McDonagh, M Nash, D Nash; D Clarke, C Carey (0-1), M Foley; M Houlihan (0-1), Seán O'Neill; Shane O'Neill, G Kirby (1-7), M Galligan (0-1); O O'Neill, Padraig Tobin, TJ Ryan (0-1). Subs: F Carroll for Seán O'Neill, B Foley (0-2) for Shane O'Neill, B Tobin for Galligan.

THE ACTION

WHAT A DAY! Knockout hurling at its best if you were a Limerick player or supporter. Knockout hurling at its most devastating from the viewpoint of their neighbours in Clare.

This was a titanic clash on the Ennis Road in Limerick, played out in front of a capacity crowd in sweltering heat. Clare entered the game as All-Ireland champions and had comprehensively beaten Limerick 12 months earlier in the Munster final.

Limerick would have felt that they were on equal terms with Clare, albeit they hadn't closed out the 1994 All-Ireland final against Offaly, when they had one hand on the Liam MacCarthy Cup.

Entering the closing minutes, it seemed that Clare had the game in their own hands if not actually won. They led by three points, but Limerick put over a flurry of points from substitute Mark Foley and Gary Kirby to drag them level. That presented Ciarán Carey with the opportunity to embark on a run, which culminated in one of the most famous points in the history of Munster Championship hurling. The Patrickswell man won it for the Tom Ryan-managed team, while Clare were left stunned, their championship over first time out.

Limerick had led by a point at half-time, 1-5 to 0-7. Their top scorer Kirby netted the game's only goal when he was placed by Pádraig Tobin. Limerick could have found the net again almost immediately, but Mike Galligan missed a good chance when in a great position.

Clare had plenty of good scoring opportunities, particularly in the opening half and not availing of most of those chances ultimately proved very costly.

Limerick won and progressed to the All-Ireland final, where they lost to Leinster opposition for the second time in three years; Wexford getting their hands on the cup.

Clare, meanwhile, took the opportunity to refocus and prepare themselves for 1997, which proved quite a year. It was the first year of the backdoor in hurling and that added a new dimension to the championship. It turned out that 1996 was the last year of win or bust championship hurling. While Clare were devastated to have lost first time out, as reigning champions they took solace in the fact that they had participated in a classic Munster championship game.

★★★★★

66

IT WAS THE hottest day I ever played a game. The tar was lifting off the road.

We came in over the brow of the hill at the Greenhills Hotel. It was jammed. The Davin Arms was packed to the ropes. As far as you could see, the place was teeming with people. It was a sea of heads. There were people and colours everywhere.

Ger Loughnane jumped up at the top of the bus.

'THIS IS THE DAY!' he roared.

'OUR FATHERS' FATHERS TOLD US ABOUT DAYS LIKE THIS!'

The hair stood up on the back of my neck.

It just hit a chord. At the right time, the right thing was said.

For all the great speeches Loughnane made to us as a group, that's the one I most remember… and more later in the dressing-room.

Even though we lost, and we had gone in as All-Ireland champions, this was the game that stood out for me and it's the one I remember most.

If you look back at the history of Clare and Limerick in the 90s… Clare shocked Limerick in 1993. They came to Ennis as National League champions, and Clare turned them over. Then in 1994 Clare were in the Munster final for a second year in-a-row and there was a lot of expectation but Limerick blew Clare away that day.

But then, they went on to throw away the All-Ireland against Offaly.

In 1995, Loughnane, Mike McNamara and Tony Considine came in. The big thing was to try and win Munster. We beat Limerick in the Munster final but they probably weren't as prepared as they were the year before. That was the signal they sent out after.

They felt that Clare shocked them in 1995, when they weren't ready. They were probably looking ahead to the All-Ireland final.

The big showdown was 1996.

Everyone was ready. We knew what was coming.

It irked Limerick to see Clare going on to win the All-Ireland in 1995. It was 1973 when Limerick had last won an All-Ireland and in '94… they had it won. They were nearly home and hosed but they lost it!

That time, there were a lot of challenge games for pitch openings, which were played in front of big crowds. In the 90s a lot of clubs were upgrading their facilities, so there was a big challenge match circuit for the opening of these pitches.

About the middle of April that year, in 1996, we played Limerick in a challenge in the Gaelic Grounds. I think it was a fundraiser for Milford Hospice and there were about 6,000 people at it. That was the interest that was there between Clare and Limerick.

It was a very heated affair that night.

I actually got sent off myself. We had been knocked out of the league and that was the last big game before the championship. It wouldn't be allowed to happen nowadays, that you would play a team you were due to meet in championship… in a challenge. But I suppose, because it was a fundraiser, Clare people would have a big tie-up with Milford as well.

There was a big build-up to the championship game.

Tom Ryan was the Limerick manager and he made some comment in the media about the Clare jersey. Whatever was said, Loughnane took it up as a slight on Clare and he maintained that the jersey had been disrespected.

We were fairly revved up, as were Limerick.

We had a training match the previous Saturday. We were motoring well and the competition for places was fairly hot. Other lads who hadn't played for Clare in 1995 were back and everyone wanted to be part of it.

On the morning of the game, we met in Cusack Park. We had a warm-up and we got the bus in to Limerick. We were really up for it… and Loughnane made a great speech before we got onto the bus.

The last thing I remember when we were going out the door of the dressing-room, Loughnane pulled out a Clare jersey from under his shirt. He was *wearing* the jersey.

'This jersey will never be disrespected!' he reminded us.

There were 44,000 people at it.

I don't think I've encountered an atmosphere like it before or since.

Limerick got off to a great start. Gary Kirby got a goal and we went in a couple of points down at half-time but we were happy with the way we were playing. I remember (Brian) Lohan jumping up at half-time and saying we were still *down* a couple of points… well and all as we thought we were doing.

Going into the last couple of minutes, we were four points clear; it looked like we were home and hosed.

It looked as if they needed a goal, but they got it back with points. Barry Foley from Patrickswell came on and he got a couple of wonder points and they drew level all of a sudden. We had missed a few scores to put it to bed.

Then they got probably the most famous score ever seen in the Gaelic Grounds from Ciarán Carey.

I'll probably be forever linked with it… because I was chasing him.

Ollie Baker was on him but Ollie had got an unmerciful blow before that. It was a wild pull and he was hit straight on the head. He had no helmet on and he was definitely concussed but the three subs were used. The blood was flowing out of him and he was probably dehydrated.

But he had to stay on.

The puck-out came down on top of Ollie and Carey. I was marking Seán O'Neill on the other side of the field. Carey caught it and I'd say Ollie didn't know where he was.

Carey started to cut straight through. I had cut across the field to get to him.

I thought I'd a great job done to catch him. He was coming in along and I was hoping someone would come to him but no-one did.

He jinked and I got caught in him when his leg came up. I ended up on the ground and he hit a great score off his right-hand side. Ciarán Carey rarely used his right-hand-side, if ever. He was a predominantly left-hand-sided hurler.

He hit it on the run. He topped it and it barely scraped over.

Fitzy could have caught it and cleared it but we were dumped out of the championship.

That time, there was very little injury time played once it hit the 70 minutes. I looked at the 1995 All-Ireland on TG4 and literally at 70 minutes, that was it. Nowadays, you could have eight or nine minutes of injury time.

It was almost the reverse of what happened to them two years earlier in the All-Ireland final against Offaly. The place flooded and we couldn't get out of there quick enough.

There was huge deflation. It looked like if we'd won the game, the year would have opened up. It was a knockout, first-round game. There was no room for error and we were dumped out.

There was devastation on the bus from being on such a high from the year before. We had seen the world as a group and now, we were gone. But I suppose it was a catalyst for what happened in 1997 and again in '98.

That's the game that has stayed with me. Ironically, we were beaten but for atmosphere, drama and a local grudge match, it was hard to top. We actually did play well too but it just didn't work out.

In a perverse way, there was nearly a satisfaction in showing that we weren't a flash in the pan. Okay, we were beaten but we were able to back up winning an All-Ireland with a really impressive performance. We didn't crumble and it was sandwiched between great years. It felt a little bit different from previous defeats, in that we had won something and there was an expectation that we could come back.

But if we hadn't come back, that 1996 game probably would have been considered a disaster.

We wouldn't have had mixed feelings about Limerick winning the All-Ireland after that. There would have been very strong feelings. The rivalry at the time was fairly bitter.

I worked at Shannon Airport for two summers with Aer Lingus. There was a huge Limerick-Clare workforce in Shannon and all over the region. I also went to college in Limerick. The rivalry was very intense. I don't think that rivalries, in general, are as intense nowadays.

I don't know why. *Is it just the modern way of looking at things?* People don't get as worked up as maybe they used to.

At that time, it was the be-all and end-all.

Maybe the backdoor has taken away some of the edge from things. Clare and Tipp had a savage rivalry at that time as well, as had Clare and Waterford.

Clare and Offaly wasn't as bitter, even though we met them a few times.

Definitely that's not there anymore. But going back to 1996, I don't think we'd have been cheering for Limerick. Definitely not. But as the years have gone on, that has softened and we'd be good friends with a lot of the Limerick lads.

When Limerick won their All-Irelands in 2018, and '20 and '21, that eased the pain for Limerick people. I saw an interview with a prominent Limerick player of that era before Clare and Limerick met in 2020. He said that they never feared Clare because they always beat us. That struck a chord with me because Clare have had a decent record against Limerick going back even to the 70s.

They came to Cusack Park in 1974 after winning the All-Ireland and Clare beat them… and Clare also beat them in 1986. The fact that Clare won the two All-Irelands in the 90s did bother Limerick people. I don't know if it bothers Clare people as much that Limerick won their two All-Irelands in the last few years.

I was very lucky to have been in the right place at the right time. It's well documented that there was a great Clare team there in the 70s, and further back as far as 1955, but they just didn't have the bit of luck that we had.

But a lot of work had gone on in the background. We had contested a Munster under-21 final in 1994 and a very good team was also beaten in the 1992 under-21 final. In 1989, the minors were beaten in the All-Ireland final by Offaly. So there was huge work being done by the clubs and by the county set-ups. Mike McNamara was involved with all of those teams.

There was really good work done so it didn't happen by accident. Then, of course, there was massive organisation. Clare brought a professionalism to it in the 90s that was copied. Kilkenny, in particular, would have based their whole game on Clare's high-intensity, high-pressure approach; huge levels of fitness and physicality.

It was a golden era, and as I say, it didn't happen by accident. Clare were the team to beat up to about 2001. They had set the standards, which Limerick are doing now.

The big difference now is diet and recovery. We finished training in Cusack Park and went across to the Sherwood Inn restaurant. You name it, we could eat it… ice cream and the whole lot. The recovery wasn't there and people weren't as aware of how to mind themselves away from the training field.

You'd have to give great credit to Loughnane, Mike McNamara and Tony Considine. Nowadays, you could have 30 or 40 people in the backroom of inter-county teams. Loughnane was the manager, he did all of the hurling coaching and he was the psychologist.

You name it, he did it.

Tony Considine also did a lot of psychology and Mike Mac, to use a modern phrase, did all of the strength and conditioning. In our time, it was running the shite out of us. He was into strength work when it wasn't even known about. A lot of those sessions went on for two hours, four or five nights a week, including running up the hill in Shannon.

It was unheard of that time. We owe an awful lot to those three men and to Colum Flynn. We've a lot to thank them for.

GER LOUGHNANE

CLARE 1-18 TIPPERARY 0-18
Munster SHC Final
Páirc Uí Chaoimh
JULY 6, 1997

A second All-Ireland final victory in three years in 1997 was all-important for Ger Loughnane (above) but nothing in his Clare managerial career compared to defeating Tipperary in the Munster final that summer.

★ **CLARE:** D Fitzgerald; M O'Halloran, B Lohan, F Lohan; L Doyle, S McMahon (0-3), A Daly; O Baker, C Lynch (0-1); J O'Connor (0-5), F Tuohy (0-1), PJ O'Connell (0-2); S McNamara (0-1), G O'Loughlin (0-3), B Murphy (0-1). Subs: D Forde (1-1) for McNamara, A Whelan for Murphy, Conor Clancy for Whelan.

★ **TIPPERARY:** B Cummins; P Shelly, N Sheehy, M Ryan; R Ryan, Colm Bonnar, C Gleeson; J Leahy (0-3), A Butler; K Tucker (0-3), D Ryan (0-4), T Dunne (0-7); L Cahill, M Cleary (0-1), P O'Dwyer. Subs: A Flanagan for O'Dwyer, Conal Bonnar for Gleeson.

THE ACTION

WHAT AN OCCASION, and yes, the game lived up to expectations.

Páirc Uí Chaoimh was wedged for what turned out to be the first of two Clare vs Tipperary championship clashes in 1997. Tipp were managed by Len Gaynor, who had filled that role for Clare prior to Ger Loughnane's appointment as manager. Gaynor had played a key role in Loughnane's time as Clare manager when he brought him in as a selector in 1994, on the understanding that the Feakle man would succeed him in the position.

That was part of the backdrop to what turned out to be an epic encounter down by the Lee.

Clare got off to a great start and dominated much of the first-half. They went in at half-time 0-13 to 0-8 ahead and Tipperary were not really at the races. Clare pulled away even more as the second-half developed. Twelve minutes from time, they led 1-17 to 0-13 and already the inquest was starting in Tipperary.

That proved a bit off the mark, though, because Tipperary outscored Clare by 0-5 to 0-1 in the closing 10 minutes and John Leahy had a great chance to equalise 30 seconds from full-time.

Declan Ryan cut a sideline across the Clare square but Leahy didn't make a full connection with his attempted pull, allowing Colin Lynch to sweep in behind him and carry the ball clear.

While Leahy missed that goal chance, Clare substitute David Forde took full advantage of his opportunity. The Ogonnelloe man picked up a break after Ger O'Loughlin had tried to evade Michael Ryan, and raced through. Forde then buried his shot into the top corner of Brendan Cummins' net. Pairc Uí Chaoimh almost went into orbit and that goal proved the difference at the end of 70 pulsating minutes.

Clare were Munster champions for the second time in three years and they had their sights set on re-capturing Liam MacCarthy come September in Croke Park.

★ ★ ★ ★ ★

❝

MICHAEL O'HALLORAN WAS on a fella called Philip O'Dwyer.

I was at the far side of the field and I saw Len Gaynor going up past the Clare dugout and down the sideline. I saw O'Dwyer moving towards him and O'Halloran after him.

'Jesus!' I said, 'I better get down there'.

O'Halloran had been involved in an incident with another Tipperary player in the league match in Ennis. I assume that Len was afraid that O'Halloran would have a dig at O'Dwyer during the national anthem or before it.

The four of us arrived together in the one spot and the band started the national anthem. O'Halloran and myself roared the national anthem into O'Dwyer's ear. There wasn't one word exchanged… and the game started.

I'll never forget that incident because it was so comical, when you think of it now. Gaynor was looking and saying, 'What the f**k is going on?" We didn't pass any comment.

We totally ignored them in one way, but we let them know that this was going to be our day.

Páirc Uí Chaoimh was like The Colosseum. You could just see the field… nothing else. The field was all you had and you had no space between it and the crowd. They were above you, rather than being away from you. That was the first day that the real link between that team and the Clare crowd was established.

Everybody realised that this was *it*. We *had* to beat Tipp.

To meet them in a Munster final, on a day like that … out on the field before the game, I'll just never forget the atmosphere but this time it was uplifting. We weren't oppressed by it.

You'd think that all of the games I played for Feakle and for Clare, and then being involved in management… you'd think it would be very difficult to pick out the game that had the greatest significance. But when it came down to it, it was no problem.

There's a lot of reasons why it stands out so much.

When you consider how important it was for the reputation of that team and for Clare as a hurling county… the atmosphere that was there that day… the display Clare gave… and the satisfaction from winning.

There is no other game that comes anywhere near.

I've always said that winning an All-Ireland is great but Mick O'Dwyer taught me the greatest lesson of all time after the 1995 All-Ireland. There was such euphoria all over the county and it gave us such prominence nationally.

I was at a function one night in 1996 and Micko was there. We were talking about matches and the place was packed. He said, 'Any team can win an All-Ireland… but it takes a great team to win two'. He said you could get lucky and win an All-Ireland. The favourites could be beaten and you could win one by chance. He said that if you could win a second one, nobody could ever question you.

He wasn't referring to Clare, but all the way back home that night I was thinking about it. He was right. If Clare had won in 1995, it would still be regarded in Clare as a brilliant year. But outside of Clare as time goes on, it would have been just a curiosity… *Remember Clare winning the All-Ireland in '95 but they did nothing afterwards.*

That kind of stuff.

In terms of respect for Clare as a hurling county, the fact that we won in 1995 made it more important for us to win another one. After being beaten in 1996, people thought maybe it was over for that Clare team.

What was worse was the league in 1997. It was on in March, April and May. We started out great in March but then we lost four games in-a-row and we were relegated. By the time the end of May came along, people were thinking… *They're gone!*

We weren't anywhere near favourites to win Munster or the All-Ireland. We only scraped over Cork in the Munster semi-final. Stephen McNamara scored a brilliant goal to squeeze us past them.

Tipperary had come to Ennis in a league match in May and they beat us by a point in a ferocious game. That gave Tipp a massive psychological boost and as well as that, they beat Limerick, who were the favourites to win Munster, by 10 points.

They went into that Munster final on an absolute high.

There wasn't huge optimism that Clare were going to beat Tipp that day. Everybody in the team knew that this was a crossroads and unless we won that day, we were back down the ladder again. If we did win, we were going to open up all kinds of possibilities for the future.

I'll never forget the bus journey down.

Daly is right… it was like an army going on a mission.

The atmosphere wasn't a bit heavy.

We went down that morning very early and we stayed in the Hayfield Manor. We had been down the week before for training in Páirc Uí Chaoimh. Tony Considine and myself had asked a taxi man to bring us to a hotel that would be nice and quiet and away from the crowd the following Sunday. He brought us into the Hayfield Manor, which was very upmarket.

We thought that there would be no hope of staying there, but we met the manager and he gave us a great deal for breakfast and rooms for the players. We wanted them to have a rest for a few hours. We used to always do that in Dublin but it was the first time that we did it for a Munster championship match.

We went down and once the players saw the place, they knew… *This is special.*

Before the game, we went down to the Mardyke for a few pucks.

Everybody seemed to be in great form. Often you'd have to rouse fellas up and you'd be watching to see who's a bit nervous or dead in themselves. They knew how significant the day was and we asked them to just give that little bit extra that day.

Once we got onto the bus, the mission had started.

They were like greyhounds in the traps waiting to get out. Rather than fearing a Munster final, which I had witnessed so many times with Clare teams, this was going in the opposite direction.

The game started at such a pace.

We should have opened up a big lead but typical of Tipp, they had a lot of players of great character on that team… Brendan Cummins, Paul Shelly, Mike Ryan, Noel Sheehy… and the Bonnars. They were tough men. Then they had the likes of John Leahy, Tommy Dunne, Declan Ryan, Michael Cleary and Eugene O'Neill… great players.

They came back into the game and it turned into a tug-o-war. They'd be on top… we'd be on top. Nobody could open a gap.

The noise!

It was just incredible that the crowd could keep up that kind of din for the whole game.

You had no maor foirne at that time.

I was the one going round the field and the other lads would watch what was going on. I'd come back and we'd have a word about what might need to be done. We were always able to make decisions very quickly.

We made decisions without any huge discussions on them. It worked brilliantly because there weren't too many people involved.

It's different nowadays when you have stats men and all of that coming into it. We had to do the stats in our heads and most of it was done by the eye. There was a great trust between the players and the four of us on the sideline, Mike, Tony, Colum and myself.

It was often in the form of a question, when I'd go out to a player... 'How do you think you're going?'

He might say, 'Leave me where I am, I'm grand!'

And we'd do that. It wasn't a question of giving orders. That trust and belief in each other was there.

There was something about those players. They could be in a frenzy in the dressing-room but they were as clear-headed and as cold-eyed as a shark when they got out on the field. They were ruthlessly cold in their decision-making.

It's very rare that you get players like that. I suppose it came from the kind of leaders that we had on the field. By pure instinct alone, we all linked in together so well on the really big days.

The decisive moment that day was when Sparrow won the ball out near the sideline. He took on Sheedy and Michael Ryan came to him.

Sparrow flicked it inside... and David Forde buried it.

I was down beside the goals when Forde scored it. The Clare crowd at the city end, Jesus ... they went up in the air and you imagined they were going to fly into the field because it seemed as if they were up above you.

Everybody was hyped to the very last.

I thought then that we would go on and win it well, but we didn't. There was great steel in those Tipperary players and they fought to the very end.

The last five minutes of that game were the longest five minutes I've experienced on a pitch. Every minute seemed like an hour. Then, of course, Leahy had a chance to equalise towards the end, when the ball didn't come up right for him.

They had another chance after that, but the referee finally blew it.

When he blew that final whistle, it was better than the All-Ireland or Munster final in 1995. It was deeper. Jesus... we had beaten Tipp in a Munster final in high summer on a fine day. That was something that most would have considered beyond Clare for nearly a century.

That is why it was so important.

It opened up a door to the future.

If we had lost that game, after playing to the absolute limit of our ability, there would be no coming back. There would have been no All-Ireland, even though it was the first year of the backdoor. There would have been no Munster Championship the following year or none of those great games we had in 1998 or '99. It was that important.

Daly was absolutely right in what he said in his speech. He was spot on. He always found the words for the occasion. He said we came down on a mission, even though we never said it was a *mission*. But he was right. We were no longer the whipping boys of Munster but the only way you could prove that was by beating Tipp, above all teams, in a Munster final.

I remember in the dressing-room afterwards, there was no shouting and I don't remember the cup being in there. But the sense of satisfaction... satisfaction is way better than euphoria. Satisfaction lasts a lifetime and the satisfaction in that dressing-room was something that we hadn't experienced in 1995.

People could look each other in the eye and say that when the challenge was greatest, against a team we all wanted to beat, we did it. There was no need to shout or no need for any jumping about. The depth of satisfaction after that is something I'll never forget.

Coming home from Croke Park with the cup was great but the sense of unity within the team and the satisfaction, I'll never forget. It was the greatest feeling

I've ever had after any game. We knew it was the ultimate test, and knowing that we had passed it was the greatest feeling you can get in sport.

There was something about that day in Páirc Uí Chaoimh.

That's the only game really that I can remember in detail. It was such a vital day for Clare hurling. That was the day that the team and the county got respect.

They earned the respect of the hurling community. Even talking about it, you're nearly back there again and you can feel the atmosphere.

NIALL GILLIGAN

CLARE 0-20 TIPPERARY 2-13
All-Ireland SHC Final
Croke Park
SEPTEMBER 14, 1997

Ger Loughnane left it to the morning of the 1997 All-Ireland final (above) before telling Niall Gilligan he would be starting for The Banner.

★ **CLARE:** D Fitzgerald; M O'Halloran, B Lohan, F Lohan; L Doyle (0-1), S McMahon (0-1), A Daly; O Baker (0-2), C Lynch (0-2); J O'Connor (0-7), C Clancy (0-1), PJ O'Connell; F Tuohy, G O'Loughlin (0-1), **N Gilligan (0-3)**. Subs: F Hegarty for Tuohy, D Forde (0-2) for O'Connell, B Murphy for Hegarty.

★ **TIPPERARY:** B Cummins; P Shelly, N Sheehy, M Ryan; L Sheedy, Colm Bonnar, Conal Bonnar; C Gleeson (0-1); T Dunne (0-5); L McGrath, D Ryan, J Leahy (0-4); B O'Meara (0-1), E O'Neill (1-1), M Cleary (0-1). Subs: A Ryan for L McGrath, Liam Cahill (1-0) for M Cleary.

THE ACTION

ROUND TWO OF an epic summer, featuring Clare and Tipperary, was staged in Croke Park.

Clare had already beaten their neighbours in that year's Munster final and if they were to hurl their way into sporting immorality, by winning a second All-Ireland inside three years, they would have to beat Tipp again.

The Len Gaynor men in blue and gold led 0-10 to 0-6 at half-time and at that juncture, it looked quite good for Tipperary, who had the breeze behind them in that first-half. Clare had made a change from the starting 15 that had been named in the days leading up to the game. Niall Gilligan was selected to start in place of Fergal Hegarty.

The Sixmilebridge man scored 0-3 from play, while another move by the management also paid off. Clare brought on David Forde for PJ O'Connell and he responded with two vital points from play.

Immediately after half-time, Liam Doyle pointed and that set the tone for a long period of Clare dominance. They were comfortably ahead entering the last 10 minutes but then Tipperary struck for a pair of late goals. Substitute Liam Cahill kicked home Tipperary's first and while he looked to be very close to the square, the score stood.

Tipperary now sensed that there was an opportunity to really go after it and they stunned Clare when Eugene O'Neill put away their second goal. Tipperary were now a point up.

Ollie Baker responded immediately with a point from play to equalise.

In an incredibly tense final couple of minutes, Jamesie O'Connor was placed by Colin Lynch and fired over what turned out to be the winning score.

Tipperary had a great chance to win it with a last-minute goal but Davy Fitzgerald made a match-winning save from John Leahy. Conor Gleeson had a good opportunity to equalise but his shot for a point drifted wide.

Clare held on to win a gripping final and get their hands on a third All-Ireland for the county.

★ ★ ★ ★ ★

"

HURLING AT THE time was just a frenzy in Clare.

My mother had passed away in 1992 and I was living at home with my father and my brother. My father passed away on February 1 (2021) and he was just in heaven for me to be on the panel at the time.

Leading up to the All-Ireland, there were banners out in Kilmurry and everywhere you went. If Loughnane was on the radio and we were working on the farm, a shout would go out to come in and listen to *Clare FM*. People lived, breathed and slept hurling at the time.

Clare people didn't go on summer holidays that time. They organised their holidays around going to Dublin, Thurles or Cork for matches.

Loughnane didn't pick me to start and it was toying in my head all week, wondering how the hell am I not starting? I had felt that I played well in the semi-final. I felt that I would be starting but you couldn't say for certain. We met on the morning of the match and we flew up from Shannon Airport.

We went into the airport hotel in Dublin and we had a major fry-up. I'd have been brought up that way. My father was an agent for a meat factory in Clonmel and we could be up at five in the morning. Breakfast would be a chop or a steak. I could have had that before I went to the airport that morning.

Keys were handed out to us then and we'd go to our rooms. I was in a room with Fergal Hegarty that morning. He had been told that he wasn't starting and he was very disappointed.

Until Loughnane had fully told me that I was starting, you still didn't want to believe. We went for a few pucks in the Aer Lingus training facility. While we were there, Loughnane called me aside and told me I was starting.

I suppose his reasoning was to take the pressure off me.

He felt that against Cork in Limerick, I didn't play well because I was down to start. I can't disagree with it because it all worked out right and I played well in the All-Ireland. That day against Cork, Sparrow was in the other corner and Conor Clancy was full-forward. I was probably the best of the three of us in the first-half but I was taken off at half-time.

But it's hard to argue with it, when it went right.

There is no doubt that the game that had the biggest bearing on my life has to be the 1997 All-Ireland final. To this day, people would often ask, 'What did you say to [Paul] Shelly?' If I was back around West Clare doing a valuation, someone would bring up something from that match.

Clare played five games in the Munster Championship and All-Ireland series that year. I actually started in four of them, whereas a lot people think that I just played in the final.

I played the full game against Kerry in the Munster quarter-final. The semi-final was against Cork and I was taken off at half-time. We were going badly and it could have been anyone but I was the novice at the time. We won the Munster final then and Daly gave the speech about the 'whipping boys'.

With Loughnane at the time, you had Davy in goals and six defenders. Those positions were nailed down… and Baker and Lynch midfield. There was probably nine forwards then rotating for six positions. Sparrow and Jamesie were the only two that were guaranteed to start… the other seven could be on or off.

Whoever started in the Munster final hadn't played well, so I started on Willie O'Connor in the semi-final against Kilkenny.

I got two or three points from play, but I still wasn't down to start the final.

That day against Tipp, I started in the right corner on Michael Ryan and with 15 minutes gone, I was going very badly. I felt that I had been fouled once or twice, but I didn't get the call.

Fergie Tuohy was on Shelly in the other corner and Shelly was dominating. Shelly had won Man of the Match twice that year and he had a bit of a reputation built up. I was moved over and I got a score off him straight away.

My dander was up then and I got another point before half-time. Rather than going in 0-10 to 0-4 down, we went in 0-10 to 0-6 down.

I was caught on camera talking to Shelly but it was only something very simple, like… *Did you see that?* I always much preferred marking that type of corner-back, who was a ball-player and a hurler. I loved marking a corner-back who'd let you get the ball and feel that he had the confidence to take it off you, rather than Michael Ryan over on the other side. He was a Michael O'Halloran type of corner-back, a blocker and a spoiler. I always found those lads much more difficult. They didn't care if they never touched the ball as long as you didn't touch it.

We were cruising until they got the two goals.

One ball bounced back off the crossbar and Eugene O'Neill finished it. Then Leahy got the ball at the end… I met him one time and he said it was often a regret that he didn't take it in. He took the shot from the '21' and Davy made a good save. It would have been some heartbreak to be beaten by two points in a game that we controlled in the second-half.

It was an emotional time too. I was still probably grieving for my mother, even though it was five years later. Michael O'Halloran had lost both of his parents too.

I remember him coming up to me after the match and giving me a hug and speaking about my mother and his parents. That's one thing that has stuck with me.

I was trying to channel it so that my mother would be proud of me and I knew she wanted me to do the best I could.

I'd often think about how life has changed. I've a wife (Deirdre) and three children now and you'd be run off your feet. That time, I was working at home on the farm and in the evenings, when my father was gone off, I'd be out in the yard pucking and maybe trying to hit a hole in the shed.

I'd tell myself… *If I can hit that, we'll win on Sunday!*

I'd be hurling away in Rossroe, in the middle of the countryside, with no-one around, only maybe a few cows looking in over the gate.

As much as I enjoyed the rollercoaster, I'd say my father did too.

When I'd come home after training, I'd throw the bag down and he'd be asking, 'Was Seánie there… was Daly there… what did Loughnane say?'

I'd be getting narky, and he'd say, 'I won't ask you any more so!'

But he was so happy that I was part of it. I often said that when we were going to Thurles or to Dublin, himself and the neighbours would be leaving before us. He'd be into the pub before it and after it for a pint and a chat. Fantastic times.

I often remember speaking to Seánie McMahon in the early 2000s. For about five or six years with Clare, Sixmilebridge and St Joseph's, there were Munster clubs, county finals, All Stars, Munster Championships and the All-Ireland.

It was just a way of life. I suppose we did understand the gravity of it but it was just the way life was. For any young hurler, you were on top of the world.

At the time, training in Crusheen and at the hill in Shannon, you thought they were torture but it was so good to be doing it too. Going to Cusack Park for a training session, with Ger Loughnane in a t-shirt, a pair of shorts... a full bag of sliotars and the sun splitting the rocks. You'd do a few drills and then we'd play a game.

Loughnane would be doing a Micheál O'Muircheartaigh on it in the middle of the field while the game was on. The intensity of it was probably harder than any championship game we played in and it always seemed to end up level. Somebody would always have to get the last score to win it. It was great to have been part of it.

I had three great early years with Clare and the 'Bridge were going well at the time too. I didn't hurl well then for three years under Cyril Lyons. It wasn't Cyril's fault. I didn't reach the heights that I felt I could have, but I did again then under Anthony Daly. Clare were just a bit short that time.

In Daly's time, we came very close but we didn't have the strength in depth in the panel. When Cork brought on a few subs, in the 2005 semi-final, we didn't have the killer blow to come off the bench.

Sixmilebridge were going through a barren spell then as well. We didn't win a championship for 11 years. We had a bit at underage but a real good crop came then from 2009 and won four under-21s. I was around 33 and I could see them winning these under-21s. In a selfish way, I was thinking... *I'm going to hold on and play a bit with these lads.*

A good friend of mine, John O'Meara, was in charge of the team and he identified that you need a couple of experienced lads to blend with the youth. He kept onto myself and Tadhg Keogh for a while.

But you have to enjoy it too. I enjoyed training and the social side of it. My wife has been very good that way too. She has always been supportive of me continuing playing.

It keeps you young. Deirdre used to be slagging me that I was going off to training with my 20-year-old friends. I'm stopped about two years now but I'm so happy that I didn't stop when I was 32 or 33. You can get old very quickly and throw in the towel.

When I was in my late-thirties, getting ready for county finals, when you have a bad game… it's very easy to say, 'I'm too old'. But I often had bad games at 23 or 24 too. You'll know yourself if you're not fit enough, or if the legs won't take you there. But if they are, one bad game doesn't mean that you stop.

When I was over teams, I used to often describe it to lads as like having a big debt with the bank. You don't have to make one big lodgement to clear out the debt. You can make small lodgements. In hurling terms, it could be a hand-pass, a hook or a block. Later on in my career, I realised that if you did enough of those things, they can get you into a game.

When you do four or five of them, you're flying it and it doesn't have to be a case of having to get a goal or a point to get back into it.

I think there are huge similarities between Clare and Sixmilebridge.

The 'Bridge's first under-21 was in 2009 and so was Clare's. Sixmilebridge went on to win four county titles and Clare won four All-Irelands. Sixmilebridge have five senior championships put on the back of that but, unfortunately, Clare have just one All-Ireland.

We could spend an hour going into those reasons.

At 43 years of age, I just wasn't able anymore. When we were doing the runs, I wasn't able to do them. In my late-thirties, I'd have been well able to hold my own with whatever training we were doing. I just said to myself that my time had come. I played intermediate in 2019 and we got to a county quarter-final. We were beaten by Broadford on penalties. Our third child had arrived and the effort for intermediate is nearly the same as for senior. I'm regraded now to junior B.

I often remind myself that I lost my mother when I was 15.

That's a loss. Losing a match isn't a loss.

Hurling is a sport and it's to be enjoyed. People have often said to me, 'Your legacy will be ruined if you play poorly in an intermediate or a junior B game'. My attitude is… *I'll play it if I enjoy it and I won't if I don't.*

As for how I finished with Clare, Sparrow rang me just before Christmas in 2009. I was 34 and I just said to him that I'd come back on Paddy's Day and he could do a fitness test with me. I said that if I was not up to it, he could get rid of me and if I was… let me play on.

He was a new manager in and he said that everyone had to do the same and that I had to start on day one. I said, 'If I start now, I'll be no good to you come May or June'.

So we parted ways.

I think he made a mistake from his own point of view. The cavalry was coming. The under-21s had won the All-Ireland in 2009 and Clare had won the Munster Minor Championship in 2010. I think it could have been so much different for Sparrow if he had played things a small bit better. I would have been happy to play for 20 minutes.

I said the same thing to John O'Meara with the 'Bridge. I used to say to him that if it was 50-50 on a call, to give it to the young lad.

In 1997, I remember the Monday morning after the Cork match. Even though we had won, I was very low after playing badly and being taken off. Whether he was being a great captain or he just wanted me to come out for a few pints, I remember Anthony Daly ringing the house phone at 12 or 1pm that day.

My father called me and said that Daly was on the phone, telling me to get up to the Halfway in Ennis. It was great fun, but fellas would go through the wall for you too. We could have gone into the pub at one o'clock that day. Jamesie O'Connor would have come in that evening. He'd have felt it a duty to go and Seánie McMahon the same… or whoever else didn't drink.

Nowadays, lads are retiring at 28 or 29.

The reason is that they're not enjoying it.

There's too much training and too many meetings. I think it's over-done. A big problem is managers being paid. They're justifying that and I think it's a huge issue for the GAA.

GERRY QUINN

CLARE 1-16 WATERFORD 1-13
All-Ireland SHC Semi-Final
Croke Park
AUGUST 11, 2002

Broken bones in his hand, sustained in the All-Ireland semi-final against Waterford, didn't stop Gerry Quinn from taking his place in the final.

★ **CLARE:** D Fitzgerald; B Quinn, B Lohan, F Lohan; D Hoey, S McMahon (0-3), **G Quinn**; J Reddan, C Lynch (0-1); J O'Connor (0-3), T Griffin (0-1), A Markham (1-1); T Carmody (0-2), N Gilligan (0-2), D Forde (0-2). Subs: O Baker (0-1) for Reddan, A Quinn for Quinn.

★ **WATERFORD:** S Brenner; B Greene, T Feeney, B Flannery; P Queally, F Hartley, E Murphy; T Browne (0-2), A Moloney (0-1); E Kelly (0-3), K McGrath (0-1), P Flynn (1-4); J Mullane (0-1), S Prendergast, E McGrath (0-1). Subs: D Shanahan for Prendergast, D Bennett for E McGrath, J Murray for Browne, M White for Mullane.

THE ACTION

IN HIS FIRST year as Clare manager, Cyril Lyons guided his county to a first All-Ireland final appearance since 1997.

Clare had been beaten by Tipperary in the Munster Championship but they then embarked on a qualifier run, which included wins over Wexford and Galway.

Waterford had beaten Tipperary in the Munster final and qualified directly for the All-Ireland semi-final. It was a first championship meeting between the counties since their 1998 Munster final clash, which Clare won after a replay. The 2002 meeting wasn't quite as incident packed as the 1998 replay.

Waterford made a lightning start and led 0-4 to 0-0 after just four minutes. Clare got back into the game and points from Tony Griffin, Colin Lynch and Seánie McMahon settled them.

Thirteen minutes before half-time, Waterford top-scorer Paul Flynn, buried a close-range free to put his side five points ahead. But just before the end of the first-half, Alan Markham hammered home a crucial goal for Clare, having been set-up by David Forde. Markham followed two minutes later with a superb point and then Niall Gilligan hit over a free, which helped Clare into a 1-10 to 1-9 lead come the interval.

Clare had the upper-hand for most of the second-half, with Tony Carmody, McMahon, Forde and Ollie Baker all firing over points.

★ ★ ★ ★ ★

66

WITH FOUR OR five minutes to go, there was a bit of a schmozzle and I ended up with a compound fracture on my hand. The bone came out, although when I looked down, I thought it was just a bit of skin.

I went to pull it off but then I saw the bone. I went down… then I saw Colum Flynn coming over from the corner of my eye. I was afraid that Colum would go putting it back in. It was fairly well out… I could see about an inch of the bone.

Colum would have popped in a few fingers for me and there were no major issues but when I saw him coming to sort out this fracture, I was trying to get out of the way.

I went off and I got some oxygen but it didn't agree with me. I was taken away in an ambulance and ended up having four pins inserted into my hand. My wedding finger was the one that came out, so the pins were inserted into the small finger, right through the hand. I had the operation that night.

It was very disappointing for me personally, in that I had been moving well and had been getting better. I had played well against Wexford and Galway, and had a decent game against Waterford. The injury was just unlucky really and I don't blame Ken McGrath.

He was their big player and was on Seánie for most of the first-half. In the second-half, he switched over onto me. I wasn't overly worried about him but you still have to be fairly cautious, so I would have sacrificed my own game to keep an eye on him.

The first 10 or 15 minutes were a bit of a haze. Waterford were moving all over the place and we found it very hard to get to grips with them. They were 0-6 to 0-1 up and they were on fire. I remember passing (Brian) Lohan and he smiled.

The message I got was that we weren't panicking.

We were still confident. Eventually, our backline really tightened up and we started to win our own personal battles. Their movement dissipated and we got into our own rhythm. Once we got going, we reeled them in fairly handy.

After that, I rehabbed for three weeks. I was at it 24/7.

Michael O'Doherty had me doing visualisation as regards the injury healing.

I went up to Seán Boylan two or three times and I was in cryotherapy a lot. I was full-time at it; two or three sessions every day. I was maintaining my fitness but I couldn't use my hands.

About a week before the All-Ireland final against Kilkenny, I started training a good bit. I met with Cyril Lyons in Toonagh handball alley and we went through a few drills. He was fairly happy that I was improving, although my hand was heavily padded and I was taking pain-killers.

We found a way to strap my hand, which was my hurley hand and I was fairly well able to function.

I went up to Dublin on the Thursday before the game to get the pins out.

The flight was at 1pm and I met the doctor at 2pm, but because I was flying back, he couldn't give me any pain-killers. So I had to get the pins out with no painkillers. He just pulled the pins out from both bones. I wouldn't have been able to play with the pins in place, so we had to do it.

I was selected at wing-back.

Was I one hundred percent fit? Definitely not hurling-wise. I didn't have the same movement in my left hand or anything close to it. The final was really disappointing. DJ's goal was a horrible one to concede and Shefflin's goal was soft as well. He got credited with it but it just tipped the outside of his hurley, spun around and into the bottom-right corner.

They were two desperate goals to concede and they kept us at a safe distance. We never fired up at all.

I ended up breaking the two fingers again, but I didn't mind once I got to play. I often wonder though, was it a distraction for the team? I played grand and they weren't carrying me but we didn't really turn up as we had against Wexford, Galway or Waterford.

I first came onto the training panel after the Munster final in 1998. I was playing minor and under-21 football at the time, but Loughnane put an end to that. There wasn't much of a choice given there. He wanted me to focus on hurling completely. I was coming into a very successful team at that stage. I really enjoyed Loughnane and I had a really good relationship with him. He was very supportive and showed a lot of faith in me.

One of the other games I most remember was Cork in the 2005 All-Ireland semi-final. It was cruel. That's the game that still haunts me, and I'd say most of the guys. Anthony Daly had come in and had done a serious job on us mentally and on our physical preparation. I never felt sharper or in better shape.

If one of us had played dead for two or three minutes, we'd have won it. I remember Davy was panicking on our puck-outs. We weren't getting the ball past their half-back line and that caused serious difficulties. It was a game that was lost in the last 10 minutes; we were on fire up to that.

We probably needed to bring a bit more experience off the bench. Anthony was trying to build a brand new team and move past the older generation. It was Galway in the final and I think we'd have had a great chance. Any day you can avoid Tipp, Kilkenny or Cork in the final, you've a super chance.

Daly brought in a psychologist and a video analyst, which I found really useful. We'd have detailed reports on who we were marking and their style of play. It was incredible detail and after the Loughnane era, it was another step in the right direction.

After that, we had a few turbulent years. It started off with the appointment of Tony Considine as manager in 2007. I was vice-captain and they dropped Davy Fitz. I took a bit of heat on that one. Davy was put out by the whole thing, as he was entitled to be from his point of view. That's when things started to spiral for me, I'm afraid.

My whole career was marred with changes in management.

I went through five or six managers. They got it right at the start when Loughnane was there. Cyril Lyons was a selector with him and then he took over. That kind of continuity was vital. Then we had other set-ups that came in off the stands really. They would have had good hurling knowledge but they came in with new ideas, such as… *These lads aren't fit enough, we'll run the shite out of them.*

Or… they're not hard enough. We'll bring them to Crusheen and get them to do push-ups in puddles of water.

It was a real mixed bag.

Dalo was another step up, even though my relationship with him wasn't hectic; although we got on great off the field. There was a psychological thing, where he felt that he had to annoy me to get the best out of me. I knew that and my ego just didn't allow me to get on with it. We butted heads a few times to the point where he was threatening to drop me and did drop me.

But my relationship with Dalo is very good and, in hindsight, he was right. I knew what he was doing and I was doing my best to go in the other direction, as you do when you're young and stupid. *Would I handle it differently now?* I would. I'd just get on with it.

Then we moved on to Tony Considine. Before we played Limerick in the 2007 All-Ireland quarter-final in Croke Park, we had to protest on the pitch for basic gear. There was a shortfall in sliotars and we had to keep using the same ones. It got really petty. To have to threaten to down hurleys on the Tuesday before an All-Ireland quarter-final was how poisonous it had become.

It was Mike McNamara after that. Mike has his strengths but I wouldn't have felt it was a progression compared to the first three managements I had hurled under. We were pretty much full-time athletes. We were working to play hurling.

Tony Griffin took a full year off from work. I wouldn't have been a million miles behind him. My work rate would have been about 30 or 40%. I was trying to live like an athlete.

When Davy came in as manager, that's when I didn't get the call back.

My relationship with Davy wouldn't have been hectic and I didn't expect a call. But not to get told either way was a little bit annoying. That is sadly for me a little bit of a memory as well; the politics that came in during my later years. When I should have been in my prime, I saw myself getting involved in GAA politics. There's no winners there and certainly not for a player.

The Henry Shefflin incident was a fairly prominent incident in my career, unfortunately. We were playing Kilkenny in the 2004 All-Ireland quarter-final replay. Shefflin came onto me. I went and caught the ball. My hurley went back and genuinely there was no malice.

If I was able to hit someone who was two or three feet behind me, with that kind of precision, I was in the wrong game. It didn't look great but there was no way that I meant it. The Clare County Board was very slow on the up-take.

I got hung, drawn and quartered on *The Sunday Game*. We sent a solicitor's letter and I got an apology on it. It went to the CCC as well and I was cleared of any wrong-doing.

I rang Shefflin the next day to explain that it certainly wasn't intentional. I started making a bit of small talk afterwards, about us [Clare] having been socialising and he took that to be disingenuous. But that wasn't the case.

I met him maybe a year afterwards and there didn't seem to be any great issue but when lads are writing books, they need things to write about, I suppose.

I was getting hate mail and phone calls.

The Clare County Board's approach was to ignore it until the following Friday. At that stage it, had been on Joe Duffy on RTÉ for two or three days. It became fairly hot and heavy. It was disappointing how Clare reacted. The story was let develop before we got anywhere close to it. By the time we made a statement on the Friday, it had blown over.

My mother Anne tells a story that, in the aftermath, my parents were on holidays in Egypt. They were sitting in an Irish bar and the next thing this lady pipes up... 'Who was that Clare thug who was playing the last day?' Mum explained who she was and there was an awkward moment but they had a bit of craic about it. It's a bit disappointing, in hindsight, the way Shefflin presented it, but I suppose people have their own ideas.

Do I think an All-Ireland medal would have changed my life? I don't. I had some amazing experiences. To go out in front of a crowd of 60,000 to 80,000 people and perform at a decent level was magical. But when I retired from hurling, I realised that I hadn't any college qualification. I was a burnt-out former inter-county player.

I went back to college at 30 to become a hotel manager. It was a five-year course, starting from the very beginning. I put my focus into that. A lot of my classmates were 18 or 19. You're going from a position where you think you're great and you have a major ego, to carrying trays around a hotel for six months. I was like a horse getting rebroken again; a fairly stubborn horse with an ego but that definitely re-grounded me very fast.

Often inter-county players can end up focusing on the past and they can find it hard to move on from where they were. It's something you can become consumed by... it's your identity. It was really important for me to focus on getting a career on track. That was the best move I ever made.

My parents were a massive influence on me.

My mother is a hurling fanatic. She was principal of Inagh National School. I'll never forget one day we were playing Knockanean in a schools game. I was 10 or 12 and my mother had this black trench coat on. When I went into secondary school at Rice College, we watched back the video of that game and the lads were asking who was that lady going up and down the line. I had to deny her.

There could be a crowd of 40,000 people and I'd hear my mother. She was quite an avid supporter. She was cleaning out her attic lately and she found seven large booklets of every paper clipping from every game that I played. I'd have to attribute my success to the culture at home. It was a very supportive environment, but there was no pressure.

The real enjoyment in playing with your county is how you get there and how you enjoyed it. Starting with Corofin, Oliver O'Loughlin was a seriously passionate hurling man and then through to John Minogue and John McInerney at St Flannan's. We never lost a game at St Flannan's. We won Dean Ryan, Harty Cups... All-Irelands.

I won a Fitzgibbon then at University of Limerick and then came onto the Clare panel in 1998. I felt that I had a great chance of winning medals but it wasn't to be. I won a few Railway Cups but they aren't what they used to be and I got a few All Star nominations but never quite got over the line.

I don't have regrets, though. I really enjoyed my time playing hurling. We trained really hard and we had a lot of good fun afterwards. I feel as an amateur athlete that it's really important to have that. You sacrifice your holidays and everything for it. It was really important for me to have an awful lot of fun during that stage. You're a young lad and you don't get that time back.

I'm glad we had a lot of craic.

When I look at the current team, do I envy them? I don't really.

I'm disappointed for them that things haven't improved and I feel sorry that Brian Lohan is dealing with a lot of political fall-out as well. There's always going to be disagreements but I think it's at a stage where firm action needs to be taken and I don't think that anything should be left off the table.

ANTHONY DALY
(& BRIAN O'CONNELL)

CORK 0-16 CLARE 0-15
All-Ireland SHC Semi-Final
Croke Park
AUGUST 14, 2005

The anguish of losing to John Allen and Cork in 2005 (above), after a near-perfect performance from his Clare team, has stayed with Anthony Daly.

★ **CLARE:** D Fitzgerald; G O'Grady, B Lohan, F Lohan; D Hoey, S McMahon (0-1), G Quinn; **B O'Connell (0-1)**, C Lynch; D McMahon, T Carmody (0-4), A Markham; A Quinn (0-2), N Gilligan (0-4), T Griffin (0-3). Subs: F Lynch for Markham, J Clancy for O'Connell, D O'Rourke for Quinn.

★ **CORK:** D Cusack; P Mulcahy, D O'Sullivan, B Murphy; S Óg Ó hAilpin (0-1), R Curran, J Gardiner (0-2); T Kenny, G O'Connor (0-2); B O'Connor (0-5), N McCarthy (0-1), T McCarthy (0-1); K Murphy (0-1), B Corcoran, J Deane (0-2). Subs: K Murphy for T McCarthy, N Ronan (0-1) for Corcoran, W Sherlock for Curran, J O'Callaghan for K Murphy.

THE ACTION

HAVING GIVEN THEIR last drop, the Clare team were simply devastated to end up losing by a point to Cork at the end of a pulsating All-Ireland semi-final.

Clare played superbly for much of this game but some poor shooting in the first-half ultimately cost them. Despite their dominance, they led by just two points at half-time.

Clare had extended that lead early in the second-half but they couldn't put Cork away. Points from Tony Griffin, Niall Gilligan, Brian O'Connell and the superb Tony Carmody put Clare into a six-point lead.

The introduction of Neil Ronan added movement and zest to the Cork attack, and that played a role in helping them to get back into it. Up to that point, Brian Lohan had been utterly imperious in his shackling of Cork full-forward, Brian Corcoran.

Clare faded as the half wore on and only put over two points in the closing 25 minutes. Still, they were two points up 10 minutes from time following scores from Andrew Quinn and Carmody.

Cork, however, had momentum behind them, at the right time and Gerry O'Connor put over the winning score to propel his side into the 2005 All-Ireland final.

There was a sense that an end of an era had been reached by Clare and, in time, that proved to be the case. They reached the last four of the 2006 All-Ireland campaign but did not replicate the ferocity and intensity of their display against Cork 12 months earlier.

In defeat, Clare lost nothing and, yet again, their many warriors showed what they were made of on the big stage. Cork went on to beat Galway in the All-Ireland final, leaving Clare to wonder what might have been. That added to Clare's frustration and sense that they had let a great opportunity slip away.

★★★★★

66

THE MOST MEMORABLE games are sometimes the ones you lost. If you win, it sits easy with you. You won that and that's nicely boxed off. But it's the ones that you thought you should have won that stick with you.

The outside world forget about it and focus on who won the All-Ireland that year. All most people remember about 2005 is that Cork hardly got out of third gear to beat Galway in the final.

After losing the semi-final, my hurt lingered for the week. The late great Peter Garvey of the Sunnybank Hotel, who was a great friend, invited me up to the second semi-final. I went up to watch Galway beating Kilkenny.

I had been consoling myself all week that we'd have to play as well again to win the final. Kilkenny were coming as well around then. I said, 'Garvey, you're after doing me worse than good'. I felt we definitely would have beaten Galway.

The rest of the world moves on. You're beaten and that's it.

We never played as well in that three years as we did in that match. We never played as well in league or championship... and that was galling.

We had got an awful kick in the chops the year before, in 2004 against Waterford. That was my first year in charge. Maybe it was inexperience. I thought we were perfect. I remember saying to (Brian) Lohan, 'What do you think of the mood?'

'Bang on, man!' he told me.

Maybe we were a bit cocky. Waterford had played very poorly in the National League final the previous week. But they went on to be very, very good in 2004. We recovered in '04 and played good hurling against Kilkenny with the sweeper. We should have nearly won the drawn game in the All-Ireland quarter-final.

It buoyed us up for the following year. We had a good league and things were knitting into place. Tony Carmody was playing the hurling of his life, Tony Griffin was on fire... Diarmuid McMahon and Gerry Quinn were flying.

We were really going well, but we got totally sucker-punched then against Tipp in Munster. I was thinking we could have won Munster. We must have missed six goals. It was torture in the rain. Tipp got two goal chances. Larry Corbett scored one and I think Michael Webster scored the other one.

There are two matches from my time, hurling and management, that stick in my craw. That's one of them... and a club match in Kerry that I was involved in. Watch that match and tell me who won, with no-one allowed to tell you the score.

We destroyed Tipp but we just didn't score.

It was described as another flop in Munster, and Loughnane had the knives out straight away. We were gutted. We did an immense amount of soul-searching.

That year, there was a group system in place for the qualifiers. We got back on track. When you're going well, you get a kick in the chops some years and you're out. We were going well, we got the kick but we were still there.

Once we got our heads around that, we were really back at it again.

We topped the group, and we got Wexford in the quarter-final. They were automatically in the quarter-final because they had got to the Leinster final. We had the beauty of the three games and you could tell that everybody was back. Waterford was the big game in the group and we beat them in Ennis.

We went up to the Temple Gate Hotel for food after that match. You could smell the atmosphere. We didn't even have a few beers. I said to the boys that this was coming hot and heavy, and that we had to take care of business. We had Dublin the following week.

I remember sitting down with Fr Harry (Bohan) and Alan (Cunningham) saying that we had a massive chance here. No-one was giving us a chance.

They were saying we were too old.

We destroyed Wexford. We had them ripped apart after 20 minutes. Still, people gave us no chance against Cork. But we knew there was a performance in us. We flew up the day before and we stayed in The Castleknock Hotel.

Denise Martin from Tyrone was doing our stats and we had Liam Moggin on board as a sports psychologist. We got all sorts of abuse for that as well. At one stage, he was called the 'mind guru' and Denise was called a 'television guru'.

Poor auld Johnny Glynn, who was our strength and conditioning coach, which he's more than qualified to be, was called the 'soccer guru'. We had to put up with all that and we kept our head down.

The night before, we had a session with Liam.

He did a bit about Muhammad Ali... and 'Rope-a-dope,' which kind of reflected people's opinion on where the match would go and that Cork would win.

We were in a great place in our heads. I prepared hard for the speech and had decided to say virtually nothing on the Sunday. That would be always my way as a manager. I'd say very little the day of the game. I was ready to come in after half an hour of Liam.

I spoke for maybe 15 minutes, which is a long time but I gave it holly.

I knew that the likes of Seánie and Brian (Lohan) probably only stayed on because I stayed on. I touched on that but I also touched on the way the younger lads had really grown into men on my watch.

I was accused after that I was loyal to the boys for too long, but as John Callinan said to Lohan afterwards, 'Why didn't you give him (Brian Corcorcan) the odd puck?' Famously, Cork took off Ronan Curran and Corcorcan.

It was nuclear for them to take off their centre-back, and remember, Corcorcan had come back from retirement. In fairness to John Allen, he showed some courage taking off his centre-back and El Sid.

The Garda escort came out to Castleknock and on the journey in on the Old Cabra Road, there were loads of Clare flags. You could sense that the supporters were back on board with us.

We hurled great stuff. They were so up for it but yet so calm.

But you have to give credit to the great Cork defence in ways. They took off Curran. They were able to bring Pat Mulcahy out from corner-back to wing-back, put John Gardener in centre-back and the sub was Wayne Sherlock.

They brought on Neil Ronan from Ballyhea and he was a completely different animal for Brian (Lohan) than Corcorcan. Brian had absolutely annihilated Corcorcan.

We were six points up with 13 minutes to go. If somebody said to me at that stage, 'Would you take this position?' I'd have said, 'We can't lose, unless we concede a goal'.

But they got two rapid-fire points… and six becomes four all of a sudden and panic sort of set in. It was torturous to watch it.

We brought on a couple of subs and tried our best to stem it.

Colin (Lynch) had absolutely ruled the roost at midfield but just couldn't get the ball to go over the bar. If we could have got the seventh point at all I'd say they'd have nearly dropped their heads a bit, but really what we needed was a goal.

Davy was in goals and there's a famous bit in the video. You're not supposed to leave the manager's area but it was down to two or three points at this stage. I ran down to the goal and he saw me coming. He knew what I was going to say.

Ó hAilpín had caught a puck-out, Gardiner had caught two and Pat Mulcahy had caught one.

'Where do you want me to f**king hit it?' he said.

I said, 'I know, I know… I'm going to bring Gilly (Niall Gilligan) out centre-forward. Try him with one or two!'

'OKAY… OKAY!' he said.

We brought Gilly out but Gardiner was on fire at that stage.

Gerry O'Connor got the winning point and he stuck his tongue out as if to say, 'This is robbery!' After that, Colin had a shot to level it but it hit the post and went wide.

I'll never forget the dressing-room afterwards.

One of the last people in was Davy and there were tears running down his face. He whaled the hurley off the ground and broke it with temper.

We'd had tears in Thurles in 1998, the '99 semi-final and the Limerick match in '96. I was young and I definitely thought I'd be Clare manager again. That was half the reason I went in that time to have a cut at it, while the boys were there.

Then do a bit of coaching here and there and go back. Obviously, it didn't pan out that way. Afterwards, I was looking over at the Lohans, Davy, Seánie, and Lynch who was cut over the head. What men! Lynch had been Man of the Match but had six shots and no score… Colin was a guaranteed two points man per game.

Gilly, who still had a good few years left, Griffin, Carmody and Diarmuid McMahon probably knew they were the future but, in that moment, the Barry Nugents and Andy Quinns were thinking, that they were sitting in a dressing-room with Brian Lohan for the last time.

I had brought Fr Harry back and they loved him. When I'd be in my manager's mode, I wouldn't talk to them. Yet people thought I was too close to the players.

But the first man I took off in the 2004 championship was my best pal Ollie Baker. I turned back to him and said, 'If you want to sulk, you can f**k into the dressing-room".

He sulked for another two minutes… and the next thing he was up with a bottle of water and he was in and out to the field doing the water with a tracksuit top on him.

That was rubbish…*Daly is too close to the players.*

But there's always going to be knives.

I did wind up staying on for 2006 and I remember going over to Seánie and Brian and saying, 'Thanks, ye don't know what ye have done for me!'

McMahon would always have been just ahead of myself and Doyler in the fitness stakes in the 90s. He would have a half stone or maybe a stone to lose some years. I made him captain and I said, 'Seánie, I'm going to need you up at the top in the runs'.

'It didn't affect you when you were captain,' he replied. 'I didn't see you up the front.'

I said to him that I had a different style of captaincy; that I had to get on with the Fingers (PJ O'Connell) and the Doylers (Liam Doyle) of this world.

I'll never forget McMahon in 2005 and '06. We used to do these one-mile runs around St Flannan's. There might be six one-mile runs in groups of five or six. Then Johnny Glynn might give them five minutes off and then the full group would go.

There was no night that Seánie wasn't in the first three of the full group. You're talking about running with lads like Carmody, Griffin, David Forde and Alan Markham… specimens!

I was talking to Jamesie and he said that we had McMahon in some shape. I said it wasn't me that had him in that shape, it was himself.

'He's mean looking… and it's February!' he said.

I would have always admired those men but my admiration for them went through the roof in those years.

"

BRIAN O'CONNELL

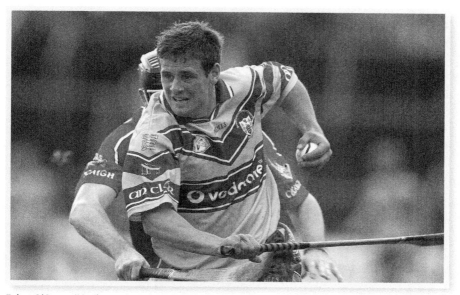

Brian O'Connell believes that the whole Clare team became consumed by losing to Cork in the 2005 All-Ireland semi-final.

"

WE WERE CONSUMED by this loss for about a year afterwards.

It's sad that when you're asked for memories from your career, you pick a defeat. That game would have meant so much more if we had won but, at the same time, it's the game that sticks out.

I was midfield with Colin Lynch. I was marking Tom Kenny, and Colin was on Gerry O'Connor. We pretty much marshalled the two of them.

Colin could have won the game on his own the same day. I'd say he's another fella that thinks about this game and twists in the bed sometimes too. He was getting onto a load of ball and in the right positions, but the finished product wasn't there that day.

I think we were five points up going into the last 15 minutes.

Being so in control of it and then for it to go pear-shaped was very frustrating. Tony Carmody had beaten Ronan Curran up a stick at centre-forward. He was causing havoc. They took Curran off and put Gardiner in centre-back, which steadied the ship for them. They also took off Brian Corcoran and brought on Neil Ronan.

The winning of the game for them was probably those two switches.

We were 0-13 to 0-8 up.

Straight after they made the change, Ronan won a ball and Joe Deane put it over the bar. The Cork crowd started getting involved and nearly straight away, they got another point. *You know the way you feel that shift?* We all recognised it and Colin actually went down to try and break their momentum. But it didn't work… we couldn't keep doing it.

I scored a point from under the Cusack Stand. It took forever to go over the bar and just dropped over by about a foot. Straight away, Donal Óg Cusack pucked it out to the other side to Gardiner, who was on his own.

I made a run to the other side of the field but he side-stepped me. I don't know if they scored out of it but I was gassed. A couple of minutes later, I was taken off and Jonathan Clancy was brought on.

There was about five minutes left. I probably looked like I was spent after making that run. I think we were two points up. It was harder to sit and have no influence on it; when you're in the stand and it's being clawed back.

Gerry O'Connor got the final point to win it for Cork. An image that has stayed in my mind was when he stuck out his tongue, looking back down the field.

I enjoyed that game so much.

It's rare enough you appreciate the game that you're in. It was low scoring but it had everything. It had the crowd getting involved… rows, good turnovers… tackles and a little bit of antics.

Brian (Lohan) and Seánie (McMahon) played on for another year but I think that this was their last hurrah. I reckon if we had got to the final, we probably would have beaten Galway.

I think we got bogged down with it. Heading into the 2006 championship, we talked a lot about that game… and then we drew Cork in the first round of the

Munster Championship.

We became obsessed.

We went up to Portumna and did a training weekend. A couple of army lads were training us for the night. It was torture. We were staying in log cabins.

We took a Friday off work and went up.

We were trekking through the woods and orienteering in small groups. We did press-ups, sit-ups, runs… one-on-one combat. Real tough stuff for four or five hours.

There were three or four buoys out in the water on Lough Derg. This was January or February, so it was freezing cold in the lake. We were in groups of five or six and one of the team members had to jump into the water and pull a box that was tied to the buoy up from the bottom of the lake.

We had to pull the box up and open it.

There was a question inside. 'What was the score in the match last year against Cork?' So that's what I mean when I talk about how we might have consumed ourselves too much with that game.

Then you had to swim from the box to a fella who was sitting in a boat out in the middle of Lough Derg and tell him the score. After that, we went off to bed.

We were wrecked.

Then some fella came in at one o'clock in the morning with the bagpipes at full blast. We had to get up again.

I loved it. The best memories that I have are from training in Cusack Park, at St Flannan's… and that kind of stuff in Lough Derg.

Later that year, about a week before either the Munster Championship or a qualifier, we were in Cusack Park on a beautiful summer's evening.

We were pucking ball before training started. It was just ourselves.

Cusack Park was empty. An announcement came over the public address system asking Seánie McMahon to come to the dressing-room.

We were like… 'What the hell?'

Seánie went in and then came running back out onto the field.

'LADS… COME ON!' he shouted.

We all ran into the dressing-room as well. The boys from the army were inside and they told us, 'We're going away for the night!'

It was a Wednesday or a Thursday night. It was a case of… *Were we part of this or were we not?* To a man, everybody got onto the bus.

It was of no real consequence to me but it was for lads who were married and had children.

We were all blind-folded in our training gear and put onto the bus. The bus went around Ennis. The music was blaring. Colin Lynch would have been able to tell us who the band were if we were able to hear him. It was really, *really* loud heavy metal… so we couldn't communicate with each other.

The bus went around Ennis a few times to try and disorientate us. They said that we were going camping out for the night.

Philip Brennan was on the panel at the time and his missus had dropped him to training. So she was in the car waiting and saw Philip and all of us going onto the bus blind-folded. She was sitting in the car, looking at this.

She didn't know what was going on… then we were all gone!

They brought us out to what turned out to be Lees Road. We were led into the forest, all still blind-folded. Your man from the army said, 'Start making a shelter for yourselves. We're staying here for the night!'

To a man, we didn't ask any questions. We started getting twigs and putting them up in a pile. They let us do that for maybe half an hour and then called us in. They said that everyone had dropped what we had and that we were clearly in this.

We didn't stay though.

We went home… but everyone had got on the bus. It was a good message.

I loved all that craic.

A lot of people would turn their nose up at that kind of stuff but, for me, when I look back on my career, it's about the memories that you make and the experiences that you have. Especially if you haven't been very successful, you have to take something from it.

When we were playing, there wasn't the group stages or the round-robin. When you lose, all you want to do is play another match. An hour later, you want to play again. Some years, we played two matches and that was it… good night and good luck.

It was cruel after a long year of hurling.

It's hard to learn what works for you when you're not getting enough games. In those years, we were crying out for the same format that was in place pre-Covid.

In 2003, Cyril Lyons was the manager. Cyril brought me in to train in about February of that year.

I played for Clare since I was about 12. Not many people would have gone through the whole underage structure. I played three years under-21.

My first senior training session was in Sixmilebridge. I was in a line of three with Lohan and Seánie. There was no introduction or anything.

You just turned up, trained and went home.

I was captain for three years… 2008 to '10. The first two years were under Mike McNamara and then Sparrow (Ger O'Loughlin) came in.

In 2008, Mike came in with Ollie Baker and Alan Cunningham but we had nobody strength and conditioning-wise. It seemed like it had gone backwards. It got frustrating then for a couple of years. It was the end of me really.

It killed my hurling and it killed my confidence. It was a tough time. I had many sleepless nights. On top of it all, I was working in the buildings and things were rocky enough there too. I was down to a three-day week.

I travelled to Australia in 2008 for the winter and when I came back, there was no job for me. Like everybody else, the builder I was working for had gone bust.

I was close to depression.

I was scared to go out. I stayed in bed for longer than I would have or should have. It was difficult because I had massive respect for Mike. When he spoke, he spoke so passionately about hurling. He commanded the room and lads listened.

When the bickering went on between him and us, it was probably to do with having had so much at our disposal previously in terms of psychology, stats, strength and conditioning… and then going down to a three-man group.

They needed to share that work and they needed somebody in to do the strength and conditioning. I went to Mike when it all started. He would have taken all of that on board, but it boiled over. It finished poorly.

I was going on 24 in 2009. I definitely wasn't equipped to deal with it. At that time and to a certain extent now if I was practising hurling, I'd be doing it very privately. I wanted to do things on my own as opposed to sharing it with anyone.

I wanted it to seem like I didn't need any help, that I was in control… and that I was captain for a reason.

I had no experience in that situation. *Should I have done something differently?* I should have tried to get people around me more.

I could, and should, have picked up the phone to people with a bit more experience. I could have picked up the phone to Seánie or to Brian, who had moved on. That would have been no problem.

I definitely could have reached out to somebody.

Maybe it might have taken a little bit of the pressure off my shoulders. There was a lot of guilt in it as well.

I didn't want to let down Mike either. He had made me captain.

I went out to him in Scariff a few times and we'd have a chat. I was trying to be a diplomat. I was trying to highlight what was wrong and trying to fix it by getting a bigger backroom team.

When Daly was there, Liam Moggin and Denise Martin were involved. Then you had Alan Cunningham, Ollie Baker and Fr Harry (Bohan). You had a bigger structure and a more professional set-up.

But it had gone too far at that stage and there was only going to be one outcome. The sad thing was that a lot of lads retired early after that. There was definitely a couple of more years in Tony Griffin and Tony Carmody.

We still had the nucleus of a very good team. 2008 was good for us.

We got to the Munster final and that was progress. We had won two games and hadn't been to a Munster final since 1999. After that, 2009 was poor and it was the first year they had talked about having relegation from the All-Ireland Championship.

We were due to play Wexford. I was on conference calls in my car with Gizzy Ling, who was captain of Wexford, Donal Óg Cusack and Dessie Farrell from the GPA, about this relegation game that we were due to be playing two days later. There was a lot going on.

We ended up having to play it, and we beat Wexford in Portlaoise. Wexford and Laois were supposed to play in the relegation final but they scrapped the idea of relegation.

After that, I started thinking… *I need a break for a while.*

I went to Australia in 2010. I was despondent about the whole thing, to be honest.

Making the decision to go back to Australia was on the back of being exhausted from what happened with Mike. My confidence was gone and I was afraid that I'd be under way more scrutiny in terms of my performance. If you're seen as playing a role in ousting a manager, you have to stand up and be accountable for it.

I was under a lot of pressure. I wasn't enjoying my hurling and I was out of work. In 2010, I told Sparrow that I was going.

I had a couple of friends playing hurling with Sinn Féin out there. I told them that I was there to just work. I was broke at this stage. My insurance was paying my mortgage at home. I got a job shuttering in the buildings.

Anyway, they coaxed me into playing in a seven-a-side tournament that happens every year in Melbourne. I was midfield and the referee threw in the ball. It bounced about two feet up and I got a pull across my left hand.

The bone split in my hand and I had to get it operated on. I had only started work the week before. I went off to the hospital and they gave me an operating date for the following week. They put it in a cast, but I cut the cast off and went to work the following morning.

I had never met the fella I was working for. It was all through an agency. I rang him and told him I needed the following week off.

I had the surgery, they put two screws into the hand and stitched it back up. I took a week off, cut the cast off and went back to work. Between all of the pulling and dragging, it never healed. It's wrecked from carrying plywood around Australia.

I came back near the end of 2011. My hip and my hand were not good. Fitzy brought me in and I joined Shannon Hibs soccer team, trying to build up fitness. I pulled my quad. The hip was causing the problems and I need a new hip at this stage.

I left the panel in April of 2013 because I just couldn't catch up. Plus, I was still suffering confidence-wise.

I'm now involved with Donal Moloney in the Clare under-16s. I got involved with the Wolfe Tones intermediate footballers a few years ago, when we won the intermediate. I went coaching with the club for two years as well, when Denis Riordan was the hurling manager. I would love to have started coaching earlier because I would have been a better player if I had coached while I was playing.

That's why I'm trying my best to go back playing junior A with Wolfe Tones (in 2021). The junior As train with the seniors and I love going down to Shannon from Oranmore, where I live now, and getting involved.

When you're coaching, you think about the game more, which I wouldn't have done while I was playing.

I'm thinking to myself that I'd love to play now… I'd do things a lot differently.

FERGAL LYNCH

CLOONEY-QUIN 0-14 BISHOPSTOWN 1-8
2006 Munster IHC Final
Gaelic Grounds Limerick
DECEMBER 16, 2006

Fergal Lynch believes himself one of the lucky ones to survive the tough times and get to taste All-Ireland glory in 2013 (above), but winning the Munster Intermediate title with Clooney-Quin seven years earlier is the one day that lives with him forever.

★ **CLOONEY-QUIN:** D O'Halloran; E Gallagher, P Markham, J O'Loughlin; A Fleming, C Duggan, E Harrison; S Conheady, C Harrison; J Earls, F Lynch (0-4), D Murphy; B Shally (0-8), R Gallagher (0-2), C Egan. Subs: S McNamara for Earls, M O'Halloran for Murphy.

★ **BISHOPSTOWN:** K O'Halloran (0-1); C O'Driscoll, M Cogan, P O'Donoghue; S O'Neill (0-1), D Crowley, B Murphy; B Cuthbert, P Cronin (0-3); K Coughlan, R Conway (1-2), J Murphy (0-1); T Murray, D O'Mahony, M Power. Subs: J O'Sullivan for Cuthbert, T O'Donoghue for Power.

THE ACTION

FOR MANY YEARS, Clooney-Quin toiled at intermediate level in Clare. Once they emerged from their own county, they were transformed. It might have been the depths of winter, but the pressure was off and they were able to hurl with abandon. Reaching a Munster club final was not on their radar at the start of 2006 but when they overcame Killanena in the county final, the road opened up in front of them.

For a good portion of the first-half of this Munster club final, it looked as if Clooney-Quin's race was run. They were slow to get going and Bishopstown were four points up after 20 minutes. The Cork champions also looked sharp at the start of the second-half and extended their lead to six points. Ronan Conway scored the Cork club's goal from about 40 metres.

However, Brian Shally put over several frees for Clooney-Quin, which kept them within touching distance of their opponents, while Fergal Lynch mined scores and frees when moved to full-forward from the half-forward line.

At the other end of the field, Cillian Duggan and Pat Markham also excelled and as the game wore on, Clooney-Quin began to really believe and their dominance started to reflect itself on the scoreboard.

Roared on by a sizeable percentage of their parish, Clooney-Quin eventually ran out three-point winners on a seismic afternoon for their club. The Christmas of 2006 was one that started early for Clooney-Quin as their year culminated in a blaze of mid-winter glory.

★★★★★

66

WE WERE SITTING in the car when there was a phone call to my father Des, who was in his first year as club chairman. The call was to tell us that the match was off due to the weather. We were due to play on a Saturday, but it was milling rain.

So I said I was going for a pint.

We went to Henchy's at around 2pm and about six players came with us. The great Bernard Gaffney, from Newmarket, came as well. He was friendly with the boys.

We went on an unmerciful session.

That night, we ended up going to town (Ennis). I remember going in with my now wife, Lorraine. We went into Ciarán's. Gaffney bought me a pint of Guinness and said, 'I bet you… you won't be able to down that!' So, of course I tried.

At 24 years of age, I thought I was going to be a hero.

So I downed it, got sick and went home. I went out the following week and as Enda Harrison said, I probably played the game of my life.

The game was on the following Sunday. Shane O'Neill and Pa Cronin are the same age as me and they were the mainstays of the Bishopstown team.

I was centre-forward and I was on a fella called Denis Crowley. Cathal Egan was full-forward for us. Bishopstown were blitzing us. They were 0-6 to 0-1 up with about five minutes to go in the first-half. I thought we were goosed and that we were going to get absolutely hockeyed.

They moved me in full-forward. I scored two points and won a free before half-time.

So it was 0-6 to 0-3 at half-time. I remember in the dressing-room we were so dejected and were wondering what were we going to do here? Conor Harrison and myself spoke to try and get us going.

We came out after half-time and scored 11 points on the trot.

The man I was marking got sent off for persistent fouling. The only scorers were myself, Ronan Gallagher and Brian Shally, who was on the frees.

I went into the dressing-room after and there were cans of Heineken and cider everywhere. It was one of the most memorable days for us. We couldn't believe that we had won a Munster Intermediate Championship.

I had been minding myself big-time because I was trying to get onto the Clare panel under Tony Considine. I had been on the panel with Anthony Daly the year before. I was making sure that I was eating right and concentrating on clean living.

Then you go out and do that the week before I played the game of my life.

Did I ever try the same approach after that? No! When you're young, I suppose you wouldn't take too much notice. But I wouldn't have tried it again, definitely not. That was the most memorable part of it. You're doing everything right and then a week before a Munster final, you lose the run of yourself.

If you're trying to play at the top level, you can't do that. It was something that luckily worked out in my favour that time. I train and manage teams now and you often see lads that would do it. You'd be giving out to them and asking them... *What are they at?* You'd be thinking to yourself, that if they knew I had done exactly that, they wouldn't be overly impressed either.

It was great for the club at the time. We had been trying to get out of intermediate for so many years. I started playing intermediate hurling when I was 15 in 1998.

We lost to Crusheen in 2000 and again in '02 to Corofin. We lost to Smith O'Brien's in 2004 and we thought we were never going to win it.

In 2006, we went on a good run and ended up beating Killanena in the final and we were senior for the first time since 1988.

It took on a life of its own after that. John McCarthy was over us and Alan Cunningham came in and started coaching us when we were getting ready for the Munster club final.

When you're winning and everything seems to be going really well and the craic is brilliant, you don't even notice that you're training hard. We were a bit nervous playing in a Munster final; we never thought we'd get there.

Along the way, we had played Éire Óg Annacarthy in the first round in Tipp town. The whole of Clooney travelled. We were after winning the intermediate in Clare and everyone was interested in seeing how we'd get on. We won that easily and then we played a team from Waterford in Ennis.

There was a huge buzz around the place because we'd had so much heartache for years. We had a mixture of youth and a bit of experience, which brought things on really well for us.

From that day in 2006, 11 years later, seven or eight lads played in the county senior final against Sixmilebridge. That Munster club win in '06 created a real bond and an affiliation to the parish. Any of us involved that day wanted to stay playing for as long as we could.

That win came at the right time. The boys were after winning the minor A final… we had lost it the year before to Inagh-Kilnamona. We had really good underage structures at the time. Cillian Duggan was only 17 and he started at centre-back that day against Bishopstown.

The following year, we never really stood up to it at senior. We were way out of our depth. We played Kilmaley, who had won a senior championship a year or two before that. We were lucky to hold on and stay senior for a couple of years until we got a foothold and were able to compete.

From my time with Clare, I particularly remember a game in Ennis in 2011. We played Limerick in the Division Two National League final in Cusack Park. Sparrow (Ger O'Loughlin) was over us. It was around the end of April. Sparrow was trying to do things as professionally as he possibly could. I felt sorry for him because some of the resources weren't there for him.

We met in Clareabbey and we were hitting off as a group for the game, in a line of cars.

I think Francis Corey was doing the garda escort.

I was the first in the line behind him. Darach Honan and Jonathan Clancy were in the car with me. He sped off and we sped off with him, but there was a line of cars from Clarecastle all the way to Cusack Park.

So some of the boys got stuck and when we got to Cusack Park, we only had two cars there and 10 players. The game had to be delayed. Francis Corey had to go back then and try to find the players in the line of cars on the way in.

That particular day took a life of its own. John Allen was the Limerick manager and he made the Limerick forwards stand in the middle of the pitch before the throw-in. We had marched around the field after the band. We were at the stand side and they marched inside us, behind no band. It was a kind of a stand-off.

Although we lost, I had a good game that day. It was probably one of my best league games for Clare.

I was marking Seamus Hickey and I scored a few points off him. Kevin Downes got a goal for Limerick from the sideline. Honan came on and scored an absolute cracker. The game was swinging from side to side all the time. We were trying to get out of Division Two and it was a very difficult time for us.

I was coming from being involved in the panel that got to the All-Ireland in 2002, along with playing National League against Kilkenny, Galway and Tipp... and then having to play Down and Carlow.

I saw the highs at the start, real lows in the middle and the highs again at the end. I was quite lucky to come out of it with something, when we won the All-Ireland in 2013. A lot of players didn't. We had lean times in the middle but, in a way, I was kind of fortunate enough to experience that.

It brought a lot of hurt and a lot of experience, that I was able to share with the lads in 2012 and '13. When you've been through it and you know what it's like, you don't want to go through that again.

The younger lads hadn't experienced the bad times. They had heard about them and might have seen them but they were so used to winning; that winning breeds winning. It was great to see that and to see them flourishing.

On the management and coaching side, I was involved with a very good county minor team in 2019 and we were unfortunate not to win the Munster Championship.

We got huge scores playing very defensively. What I was trying to do was create as many opportunities as we could for our best players.

Either way, I was going to be criticised, no matter what way we played. If we were going to get hammered by 20 points and play open hurling, we were going to get criticised. But it was very enjoyable and it brought players along. Most of them went on to win a Harty Cup with St Flannan's, which they hadn't done for years. Brendan Bugler and Kevin O'Grady carried on the work that we had done and it's good to see that there are really good players in Clare.

There was no way we were going to be able to compete with any of those teams in Munster by not setting up the way we did. We beat Cork, who had been tipped to win the All-Ireland in 2019. We beat them in Cusack Park to knock them out and to get to a Munster final. We wouldn't have done that only for the way that we played.

We're at a crossroads in Clare in terms of where we're going with coaching and players. I'd love to be able to come back and be involved in Clare at some level but I don't think that it's going to happen until things change.

All we really need to do is focus on their development. Sometimes we get caught up in stuff outside of that. We all know that there are problems and it's up to other people to sort them out. But the focus should be on the players and their development.

That said, there is a good bit of work being done at underage. I'm currently with a senior team in Galway (Castlegar) who have great potential. It's about trying to mix the experience with the youth.

Every part of the country you go to, there's always a GAA club or a pitch somewhere. We have our identity in our parish. We'd class ourselves as a country club and we'd be very proud of that. There's back-biting and in-fighting in every club but when you throw on the jersey and go out, you're all the one.

It's a few years ago now, but I'll never forget that day in 2006.

Every club needs a year like that to keep things going and to keep the fire burning. We got to experience it that year and hopefully we will again.

CIAN DILLON

CLARE 3-23 GALWAY 5-15 (AET)
All-Ireland U-21 HC Semi-Final
Semple Stadium Thurles
AUGUST 22, 2009

Cian Dillon (above, in action against James Nolan of Kilkenny in the 2009 All-Ireland under-21 final) believes his debut performance against Joe Canning in the semi-final that year was the making or breaking of him as a Clare hurler.

★ **CLARE:** D Touhy; J Gunning, E Glynn, C O'Doherty; D O'Donovan, N O'Connell (0-1), P O'Connor; E Barrett, C Chaplin; J Conlon (0-3), C O'Donovan (0-1), S Collins (0-2); D Honan (2-4), C Morey (0-1), C Ryan (0-8). Subs: **C Dillon** for Gunning, C McGrath (1-1) for O'Connor, C Tierney (0-2) for Morey, P Kelly for Collins.

★ **GALWAY:** J Skehill; S Quinn, C Daly, M Dolphin; D Connolly, B Regan, C Forde; D Burke (0-1), S Óg Linnane; K Keehan, A Harte (1-2), E Forde (0-3); A Dolan (0-1), J Canning (4-7), N Quinn (0-1) Subs: K Killilea for Dolan, B Daly for Linnane, G Burke for Teehan, J Ryan for S Quinn, Linnane for Forde.

THE ACTION

THIS HAD EVERYTHING. Superb scores, great defending, missed opportunities and an enthralled crowd. The attendance of almost 6,000 got value for their money, leaving Thurles with memories of a classic encounter, etched forever in their thoughts.

Clare had just emerged from Munster, having won their first provincial title at this level, while Galway availed of a place as the Connacht representatives in the All-Ireland semi-final.

This game turned into a shoot-out between Joe Canning and Darach Honan, with both contributing several moments of pure class.

Clare equalised at the end of normal time and forced extra-time, which was equally epic. At the end of normal time, the scoreline read Clare 2-16, Galway 3-13.

Canning put away four goals in total, the fourth of which put Galway into a one-point lead, close to the end of extra-time. Late points from Honan and Colin Ryan won it for Clare following an enthralling 80 minutes of hurling.

While the goalkeepers had to pick the ball out of their net eight times between them, Donal Tuohy and James Skehill also made several outstanding saves, which contributed hugely to the entertainment and excitement.

Clare had many heroes but the most impressive facet of their display was that they didn't panic. Previous Clare underage teams, who were often equally talented, regularly didn't produce what they were capable of when the pressure came on.

Having struggled for so many decades to emerge from Munster, it seemed that once Clare managed to achieve that, the shackles were off. They went on to defeat Kilkenny in the All-Ireland final, winning the first of four under-21 All-Irelands between 2009 and '14.

★★★★★

66

MY FIRST GAME at any level for Clare was the crazy under-21 All-Ireland semi-final against Galway in 2009.

I had been injured for the whole Munster Championship with a broken foot.

Crusheen had a Clare Cup game the week before the Munster semi-final against Limerick. The under-21 management didn't want us to play club and I don't think the game meant too much, but we were never going to pull rank and say we wouldn't play.

With about 10 minutes to go in the first-half, I went up for a ball and came down on my foot. I was hobbling around for a minute or two but the physio told me to come off quick and get it iced.

The under-21 management had said to go and play the game but that they were training at the same time. They said to come in for the dinner afterwards, so that they could make sure we were all right.

We had four lads on the panel at the time… Ciarán O'Doherty was captain, and Donal Tuohy and Joey Meaney. I didn't know what to say to management and I was hoping it would be all right in a day or two. I didn't want to say much but Alan Dunne, who had been involved with Crusheen a few years previously, had got on to one of the Crusheen selectors before we landed in. He was told that I had taken 'a bit of a knock'. The next thing, they saw me hobbling.

I went to Ennis hospital and got it checked out. I was there for four or five hours and I didn't get home until about 3am. The broken foot was confirmed… I was told that I'd be out for six weeks.

I hadn't played for Clare yet, but it was fairly certain that I'd have been starting full-back. I hadn't played Clare minor - 2006 was my last year minor and I didn't make the squad. I didn't make the Harty panel in St Flannan's either.

But my first year senior with Crusheen in 2006 went well and we got to the county final the following year. In 2007, I was called into the under-21 panel, in my first year out of minor. It was a weird trajectory. I was thinking that I didn't belong there at all.

The following year, I was called onto the Clare senior panel, having not played under-21, apart from a few challenges.

When I was called into the senior panel, I rang Mike McNamara, the manager at the time. Within two weeks of the county final, I had received a letter saying that I had got the call. That was early November 2007. When I rang him, I said I hadn't played Clare under-21 or Clare minor.

He said they wouldn't have called me if I wasn't good enough, and to come in and see how I got on.

So I went through the slog in November, December and January. Absolute slogging… Ballyline and everything you could think of from what the boys were doing in the '90s. All that craic.

There was a group of us in NUIG saying… 'Will we go to America?'

I jumped at it.

I knew that I wasn't going to be playing Clare senior hurling, having not played anything beforehand.

So my second year of under-21 was me going to America. About five or six of the panel that won the All-Ireland the following year were there with me. We all missed that 2008 Munster final… Donal Tuohy and the puck-out controversy. The O'Donovan twins, Enda Barrett, myself and Bernard Gaffney were in Chicago on a J1.

We could tell that the under-21 management weren't happy about it, but lads have to live their lives too.

We were watching it all and hearing about the controversy. We couldn't believe the way it ended. I think a few Crusheen followers were scaling the fence in Cusack Park, to make sure the referee knew about the '65'.

So 2009 was my first year to play for Clare.

We had the same under-21 management from 2007 to '09; John Minogue, Alan Dunne, Cyril Lyons and Seán O'Halloran. When we met in '09, Alan Dunne had a good gripe about lads going off to America. Our first meeting was in the Temple Gate Hotel. Enda Barrett was wearing a White Sox or Cubs baseball cap and Alan took a disliking to that straight away.

He said that we owed them one after the year before. We knew that we had to get the head down and train hard.

Even then, we were only hoping that things would go right for us. There was no tradition of winning anything. We were training at St Flannan's a good lot and if we were getting 15 lads out, we were going well.

After the club under-21 competitions, you'd have Clare Cup cutting in and then you'd have some lads half on the Clare senior panel. We were getting poor numbers and we called it out with management.

'Where was everyone and are we going to try and get something going here… or what?'

It got to the middle of May before we started getting proper numbers and started training hard. We played a few challenges and started to get momentum. We knew we were in good nick going into the Munster campaign, and then I got injured.

The Munster final was three weeks after the Limerick game. We were playing Waterford below in Waterford.

I'd been in the boot six weeks at that stage. Management hadn't given up hope that I could come right for it and I was loving hearing that. That was massive because my involvement with Clare up to then had been very chequered. But I could see that they did value me and they did communicate it, which did a lot for my confidence.

I was turning 21 that year and hadn't hurled for St Flannan's or for Clare. I had played a year or two of Fitzgibbon but our team wasn't hectic. Nothing can replace the cut and thrust of championship and I hadn't experienced it.

The fact that they rated me to think about putting me in, knowing I wouldn't be fully fit, even that gave me the confidence that I could do this.

So I was trying my best to do whatever I had to do.

There's a cold water spring on a bad bend, up in the mountain, in Ballinruan. I'd sit on the ditch and throw the legs in. I was going up there doing that.

For the Munster final against Waterford, there was a plan put in place for me to get an injection in the dressing-room and to do a disguised warm-up, with a few lads, before the team warm-up.

I had even kept it under wraps from the family. One of the brothers texted me asking was I thinking of going playing?

Three subs were picked to go out with me. All of us had the helmets on and I was doing a few sprints and turns. I was able to run but I couldn't stop, turn and power off. I can safely say that if I had played, I'd have been cleaned out the gate and I'd probably have never hurled for Clare again.

The warm-up lasted about 10 minutes but it didn't work. I remember getting the boot strapped back on me and I watched the game. It was a tight match but we won and I was hobbling on the field, way behind everyone, to join the celebrations.

It just about came right for the Galway game. There was three weeks from the Munster final to the Galway game and if it had been two, I don't think I would have made it.

The week before the Galway game was my first time training. The match was on the Saturday and we trained the previous Sunday in Cusack Park. We trained in Thurles the same week and I got through that fine.

The night before the match, Alan Dunne and John Minogue came out to Crusheen. They said they'd make a call on me the following day. I knew I wasn't going to start but I wanted to make sure that my hat was in the ring.

One of the club lads happened to be there and he pucked balls to me. I was turning at cones and the touch was good. They were very happy with it and they said that I'd probably be coming on. I prepared for the game because I knew it was going to be my first game for Clare.

I was looking forward to it too and I felt calm.

A recording of the game was on TG4 during the lockdown in the summer of 2020. A lot of lads would have said to me…'Only for you against Joe Canning that day…'

I hadn't watched the game really since but when I watched it, Canning actually won a fair bit of ball off me. I thought that any ball that came up, I had won them all but he caught two or three balls. He set up a score and dispossessed me once.

For me, it was definitely a game of significance rather than the best performance ever. I was called in after 20 minutes. Galway were looking very dangerous in that first-half. Canning had scored 1-2. Eamon Glynn was full-back and he had done well on him but in the space of a couple of minutes, Eamon had given away a 21-yard free and Canning had slotted it. Then Eamon got a yellow card, so I was brought on for James Gunning.

They kept me in the corner for a minute or two, which I remember being a shrewd move. If you send in a lad for his debut, put him over on Joe Canning straight away and he loses the first ball... *Goodnight!*

It was very shrewd. Within the first minute or two, I got a pass and cleared the ball. I felt that I settled in straight away.

Joe had just stuck a penalty and had now scored 2-2. We were down four points. Once he scored the penalty, management said to go over on him. I had about five minutes to battle with him before half-time and that went fine.

At the start of the second-half, I won a free off him in the first minute. A high ball came up between us. I got a step ahead of him and put up the hurley. He played my hurley and the ref gave me the free but nine times out of 10, he gets away with that and he's in behind me. All of a sudden, they're up seven points and my debut has gone downhill fast.

It's fine margins. Thankfully, I got the free and Darach Honan ended up getting a goal. We're now only down a point and my second-half has started great.

You could clearly see that their tactic was to hit the ball into Joe, he was causing so much bother.

But in the moment you don't think the worst and you think about shoring it up as best you can. The lads around me were flying and we were hurling well.

He was kept full-forward the whole time and he hit 3-7, all from dead balls. He scored two sidelines. Himself and Honan were just immense.

Any time that Honan got a ball, the roar that went up was insane. He was on a different level and Canning was the same, in fairness.

I fared reasonably well in that there was no time when he won a ball off me and took me on or where I made a bad mistake. I won some ball off him and tapped ball away, which stopped him doing what he had been doing previously. But there was definitely one or two moments, considering my experience of senior now, that I wouldn't dream of doing.

I gave away one free on him and I thought it was awful harsh. The ball went in behind the two of us. I was half a step ahead of him and I put my arm across. He did the same to me but the free was blown and he knocked it over.

He was still doing sublime stuff but I was happy with how I was marking him.

It was Honan vs Canning... but the two goalies were immense altogether.

Ciarán O'Doherty got in two savage hooks. Both were point-blank goal chances. Proper last-ditch stuff. The game could have been out of sight for either Galway or Clare before I even came on.

I know I hadn't trained much but I didn't feel any tiredness. It might have been different if I had started the game and then it went to extra time.

Towards the end of the second-half, they went ahead. Conor Tierney came on for us and got a point straight after that. We always had an answer for them, any time they got a score. At the end of normal time, we were the ones who equalised and we felt that it was a second chance for us.

For a lot of the lads who had experienced the misery of 2008 in Cusack Park and having it robbed from them, they felt that this was our chance.

We got the dream start to extra-time. Honan got a goal but then they responded with a goal and Canning put over a sideline.

We were two points up with about four minutes to go.

James Skehill came out from goals to take a long-range free. I remember the conversation explicitly. We knew it was going to go to Canning so we got bodies back. Enda Barrett and Ciarán O'Doherty came back on the goal-line with Tuts.

Everyone was being marked... I was on Canning.

I had time to say 'Will I go with the hand or the hurley?'

I remember Enda Barrett behind me saying, 'Dillon... up with the hurley and just clear it out!' That made up my mind.

It landed around the 14-yard line. I went up with two hands on the hurley.

I was right beside him. He gave a flick, connected and it was in the goal.

I couldn't believe it. I had been thinking that I had done well on this lad.

He had been causing trouble but he hadn't scored from play at all in 60 minutes of marking him. Next thing, he pops up with an outrageous goal.

They were a point up and they were absolutely gone cracked.

But we responded well. Conor McGrath got a point straight away, Colin Ryan put over a long free and Honan got a ridiculous point from the sideline. He stood up and from a tight angle, 15 yards out, put it over the bar.

The lads saved me.

I can look back on it now, having played nearly 10 years with the seniors, and be happy with my lot. But if that game hadn't gone well for me, I mightn't have made the Clare senior team at all. The club didn't go well that year and I didn't play well after coming back from the under-21s.

If that game hadn't gone well for me, there's a fair chance that I wouldn't have been on the senior panel the following year.

There would have been no under-21 All-Ireland, which was a massive thing for the county. A lot of us came onto the senior panel the following year. We came in expecting to be at the top table. Not in an arrogant way, but we wanted to prove that we were good enough. The older players fed off that.

Playing Kilkenny in the under-21 final was massive for our own confidence. We didn't fear going up to Croke Park, nor did we fear Kilkenny. A lot of it was the hurt that the lads had from the previous year in the Munster final. It was made for us.

I can definitely say that it was the most significant game I ever played for the county. You don't get to replay your debut.

PODGE COLLINS

CLARE 0-17   TIPPERARY 1-13
Munster MHC Play-Off Round Two
Cusack Park, Ennis
MAY 5, 2010

Podge Collins celebrates scoring against Tipperary in the Minor Championship in 2010.

★ **CLARE:** R Taaffe; P Flanagan, N Purcell, S Morey; E Boyce (0-1), K Lynch, S O'Halloran; T Kelly (0-2), C Galvin; A Cunningham, **P Collins (0-4)**, J Shanahan (0-1); C O'Connell, N Arthur (0-7), D O'Halloran (0-2). Subs: H Vaughan for Purcell, A Mulready for O'Connell.

★ **TIPPERARY:** D Reddan; C Barrett, A Ryan, J O'Dwyer; L Treacy, B Stapleton, J Meagher; J Forde (0-1), D Flynn (0-1); D Butler (0-1), N O'Meara, L McGrath (1-3); M O'Brien (0-2), A McCormack (0-2), C Horan (0-1). Subs: T Heffernan (0-1) for Forde, J Cahill (0-1) for Butler, D McCormack for Horan, P Dalton for Heffernan.

THE ACTION

THIS WAS KNOCK-OUT championship hurling. Clare entered their Munster Minor Championship play-off against Tipperary having lost to Waterford and beaten Kerry. Tipperary had been beaten, after extra-time, by Cork in an epic.

This was last-chance saloon for both teams. For the victors, their reward was a Munster semi-final meeting with Limerick, while the losers' inter-county season would grind to an abrupt halt.

Tony Kelly won it for his county with a late point and, from there on, the 2010 Clare minors grew and grew. They won the Munster Championship, beating Waterford 1-16 to 1-11. It was Clare's first provincial minor title since 1989. They went on to reach the All-Ireland final, where they lost to Kilkenny.

On that May evening in Cusack Park, Clare had started well and led 0-4 to 0-1 after just 11 minutes with points from Man of the Match Podge Collins, David O'Halloran, Niall Arthur and Enda Boyce. They remained in front, leading 0-7 to 0-6 at half-time.

However, Tipperary had John Meagher and Joe O'Dwyer excelling in defence. Losing Jason Forde to injury was a big blow, but they started the second-half well and led by a point 10 minutes into the new period.

Enda Boyce and Kelly then began to dominate and six minutes from time they had Clare in a decisive position, leading 0-16 to 0-11. *Or so it seemed.*

Boyce was sent-off on a second yellow and it was then that Liam McGrath struck for a superb Tipperary goal. Niall O'Meara equalised a minute from time, and extra-time looked inevitable.

As he did so often subsequently, Kelly found a way and fired over a magnificent winning point.

The Clare minors' summer now stretched ahead and culminated in Croke Park on All-Ireland final afternoon.

★★★★★

66

ONE OF THE reasons I remember the day so well is because of the amount of people who said they weren't going to the match.

So, I wasn't too optimistic in the days leading up to it.

The fans who did go were really die-hard Clare supporters. I had heard people talk about the rattling of the sheds in Cusack Park but that was the first time I experienced it.

I remember having goosebumps on the field. It was a close game and we went a point up near the end. For a game that's so long ago, it really stuck with me.

The bookies had us at 10/1 because of the gulf in previous results between ourselves and Tipperary at underage. People were saying that they didn't need a ticket for the game because they didn't think it was going to be too close. *I wasn't arguing with them.* We had lost to Waterford in the opening game, which is a game that I remember nothing about. Paraic Mahony and Darragh Fives were playing for them that year. We beat Kerry, and then we had Tipperary in Cusack Park. They were probably favourites to win Munster.

After beating them, we went on to win Munster and we got to the All-Ireland final where we lost to Kilkenny.

I wasn't involved in my age groups at under-14 or under-15. At under-16, I made a small breakthrough and then I was called into the minor panel when I was 17.

I hit four points against Tipperary that day, but I wouldn't have been known on that team for scoring. It wasn't that I was particularly good that day, either. We just had a good balanced team.

Tony Kelly was his usual self, even as a 17-year-old playing minor. Colm Galvin and Tony at midfield were an unbelievable force but what really made that team was how competitive training games were.

A player like Darragh Corry was centre-back on the second team at training. I couldn't puck a ball off him. Cathal Doohan was playing wing back and wing forward. The training matches were absolutely *animal* and there was never more than a point or two in them.

Then when you're selected on the team, you're feeling extra lucky to be playing because it's so competitive to get on the first fifteen.

Donal Moloney, Gerry O'Connor and Paul Kinnerk were over us. They really gave us the best chance to succeed. They didn't want anything else to be a worry for us, apart from going out onto the field to train and play. And to be happy doing it.

As competitive as those matches were, you'd often leave frustrated because you didn't puck a ball off your man. Training was very enjoyable though. I've had some great coaches at underage but from the first to the last minute, we were all *competing* in training in some way, shape or form. That definitely stood to us.

Our 2010 minor team had a special bond.

Óige Murphy would have been slagging me about my 'minor friends' because we were so close at that point. And that was before *The Inbetweeners*!

There was a serious bond there. You're at an age where you don't have a lot of responsibilities. You're doing your Leaving Cert and life hasn't really come at you yet. You're just thinking about your hurling, and having a bit of craic. Hurling was *our* craic; that's what we got the most fun out of at that time.

One thing we never had was an inferiority complex. From Cratloe with Joe McGrath and Colm (Collins); in school with Ger Keane, Alan Cunningham and Colm Hanley; up to minor with Donal, Gerry, Paul Kinnerk and Michael Considine in the football… they drilled that into us.

Donal Moloney probably addressed it head-on in that he thought that Kilkenny were the best minor team in Ireland at that time. So we played three challenge games against them in 2010. We also played Cork in Páirc Uí Chaoimh.

The message was that we were on a par with them. It was similar with the minor footballers that year. It was ingrained in us that we were going to beat Cork. We didn't, but it wasn't because we didn't think we were good enough.

Losing to Cork in the football, in Cusack Park, is also one game that I remember very well. We should have beaten them, and they went on to lose to Tyrone in the All-Ireland final. They picked the ball off the ground on the 21-yard line going into injury-time. The referee didn't give it and they kicked the last three points to win by a point or two. Michael Considine was over us that year. As regards Clare, those two games really stuck with me.

I couldn't get rid of those memories if I tried, whereas from 2010 on a lot of stuff blurs together.

On a broader note, the 2009 under-21 All-Ireland win really spurred on the whole county. They beat Kilkenny in the final and it was a wake-up call for Clare. They beat Galway in the semi-final. Joe Canning was playing for Galway and they had *some* team.

I really feel that Clare team was the catalyst for what followed.

Also in 2009, I came on for Cratloe against Broadford in the Clare Senior Hurling Championship quarter-final.

I played a junior club game in Clareabbey before the senior game on the same day.

I wasn't on the senior panel as far as I knew, even though I was named on the panel in the match programme. Mike Deegan came up to me after the junior game and said, 'You're going to Cusack Park now!'

We drew with Broadford that day. I came on with a few minutes to go and, luckily enough, a Damien Browne free came off the crossbar. I doubled on it and put it over the bar to equalise. It went to a replay.

I wasn't too nervous coming on, to be honest. You want to play and when you're younger, you think about it a lot less. Lads that you really look up to, people like Barry Duggan and Seán Hawes, when they come up to you after the game and you see how much it meant to them, it sinks in. I only came on for a minute or two in the replay.

We won the replay and we beat Kilmaley in the semi-final. I don't think I came on but I got a cameo in the county final against Clonlara. It was like... *Thanks for getting that point against Broadford!*

On the dual-player issue, I'd like to think it is possible to play both up to minor and under-20. I'd love to believe that *the call* should be left to the players.

If they want to play for Clare in hurling and football up to under-20, I don't think that any manager should be allowed to tell a child or a young adult that they can't play both.

When it comes to senior, and the level that it has gone to, missing one training session is detrimental to the information you're going to get prior to a match. I definitely found that in my last year trying to play dual.

It was just a waste of time. I was arriving to training not knowing which positions I should be taking up. If there was a call, I wasn't sure what it was.

I was trying to be as organised as I could, but I just wasn't getting the information. It's not achievable at senior.

When you specialise in one sport, you train for six months and play matches for maybe two or three months. That can be taxing enough, whereas if you had a pre-season and six months of games, split between the codes, the season would be a lot more enjoyable. But that's not how it works. You end up with clashes and it doesn't appear that the GAA accommodates dual players.

Everyone wants to be successful and a manager of a GAA team is no different. They want their team to be as successful as possible, not only because it reflects well on them but it reflects well to the parents of the children.

I'd love to think that if a child did want to play both, that they would be accommodated. Maybe I'm an idealist!

Between school, Cratloe and Clare, I've been lucky enough to have had some great days in hurling and football, all equally enjoyable.

Actually, a game that I remember from club football is one against Liscannor back in Cooraclare. It was really the start of our group. We had a really young team. We had heard a lot about Liscannor and how hard they were to beat.

We'd had a game the weekend before it. People seemed to think that we might have the legs on them but that they would have the edge physically. It was one of the toughest championship games that I've ever been involved in and to come out the right side of it kick-started us at senior. We learned how to get rid of the ball quickly and move!

Winning the All-Ireland in 2013 was, of course, a huge highlight.

Something from the drawn All-Ireland against Cork, that I remember and regret, was when the ball hit the post and I went to kick it.

Anthony Nash came sliding out, and they went down the field and got a goal. It was a six-point swing. I should have knocked it out of my mind straightaway but it stuck with me for a week after the game. *I couldn't get rid of it.*

If I was to go back and give myself any bit of advice, it would be to park things like that.

I remember Conor Ryan's performance from the drawn game. Seamus Harnedy was a player that we had been talking about in training the week before the game.

I remember thinking during the game that Conor was having a special game. I didn't play as well in the replay. Brian Murphy was marking me. I remember coming off and I had a perfect view for Conor McGrath's goal.

I had been travelling up and down from Cork with Shane O'Donnell all year. I probably got his place for the first game against Cork in the Munster quarter-final, which we lost. Shane had been sick before the game... and I managed to hold onto my place.

We were competing for a spot on the team but we were the best of friends off the field. When you're that close to people and you see the performance he gave in the 2013 replay, you admire and cherish those times.

You do think back at the lack of success that followed. No matter what you do, you always want more but, unfortunately, so far we haven't done that.

It's a hard one to put your finger on. You hear of teams around the country that might have enjoyed themselves too much or who didn't train enough. For us, that couldn't have been further from the truth.

Different people were brought in to try and bring us on. I'd be very disappointed that we didn't kick-on and win more, but I do feel that the players put in a big effort every year. I'd find it a lot harder to swallow if we hadn't put in the effort every year and we fell short because of that. I don't think that was the case.

But I do feel that the team came on a lot in 2021 and they have given themselves a platform to build on.

At the moment, I'm fully pledged with Cratloe hurling and football. If you're not performing well enough in the club environment, confidence wouldn't be great and you wouldn't feel like you can offer anything beyond that. So that's my priority.

I'm a terrible spectator. I get way too involved watching games and sometimes I have to sit by myself. I just want the best for Clare and for Cratloe. Anytime I'm not playing, that's what is going through my head.

I wasn't involved with the Clare hurlers this year (2021), but if they had won the All-Ireland, I'd be trying to hop the fence and get onto the field after the game! I grew up supporting Clare and that has never left me.

Whoever has the jersey on will always get my support.

BRENDAN BUGLER
(& PAT O'CONNOR)

CLARE 1-16 DUBLIN O-16
All-Ireland SHC Qualifier
Cusack Park
JULY 7, 2012

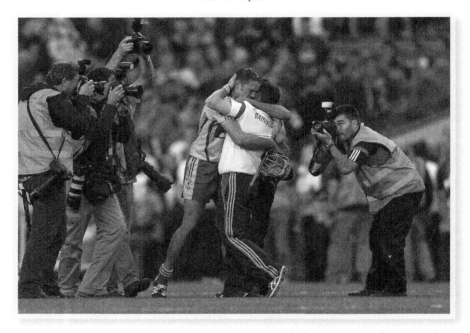

Brendan Bugler celebrates with Davy Fitzgerald at the end of the All-Ireland final replay in 2013, but he believes if Clare had not ended their mini-famine by beating Dublin the year before, then the Liam MacCarthy Cup in '13 might have eluded them.

★ **CLARE:** P Kelly; D O'Donovan, C Dillon, C Cooney; **B Bugler**, P Donnellan, N O'Connell; S Morey (O-1), S Collins (O-2); F Lynch, J Conlon (O-4), J Clancy; T Kelly (1-2), D Honan (O-2), C McGrath (O-5). Subs: P O'Connor for Cooney, C Galvin for Clancy, C Ryan for Honan, A Cunningham for Lynch.

★ **DUBLIN:** G Maguire; R Treanor, P Kelly, N Corcoran (O-1); J Boland, T Brady, M Carton; J McCaffrey, M O'Brien (O-2); L Rushe, A McCrabbe (O-1), D Sutcliffe (O-1); P Ryan (O-9), R O'Dwyer, D Treacy (O-1). Subs: D O'Callaghan for O'Dwyer, S Durkin for McCaffrey, N McMorrow for Ryan, S Lambert (O-1) for O'Brien, R O'Carroll for Treacy.

THE ACTION

FOR CLARE, THIS game was all about the result. The performances could wait. Since reaching the 2008 Munster final, Clare had not won a championship match bar a relegation game against Wexford in 2009.

That's not to say there wasn't immense hope on the horizon. It was clear that a very talented group of young hurlers were coming through from the under-21 and minor teams, that had won provincial titles and contested All-Ireland finals.

Still, Clare needed to win a championship game to back up the fact that they had won promotion from Division 1B in Davy Fizgerald's first year as manager. Throw in the fact that two-time Clare All-Ireland winning captain Anthony Daly was in the Dublin dug-out and it added immense interest to this game.

Cusack Park was full but for a while the home supporters were almost silent as Dublin raced into a six-point lead. Clare were also a man down when Nicky O'Connell was sent off on a double yellow card. It was looking grim for a Clare team that had an average age of 22 and featured a championship newcomer in Tony Kelly.

The Ballyea man goaled from a 20-metre free, 18 minutes into the second-half, and that goal helped Clare into a 1-13 to 0-14 lead. The Clare players drew energy from a very vocal home crowd in the closing quarter and they held on to record a badly-needed and morale-boosting win.

Dublin had won the National League title the year before, but they disappointed in 2012. A bit like Clare, they enjoyed a much more productive 2013, winning the Leinster Championship and narrowly losing to Tipperary in the All-Ireland semi-final.

John Conlon and Brendan Bugler played very well for Clare in the 2012 qualifier win. They went on to play and lose to Limerick in the next round.

★ ★ ★ ★ ★

66

IT'S ONLY LOOKING back that you wonder would 2013 have happened at all if we hadn't won that game against Dublin? That's how big it felt for me.

I'm convinced that if we hadn't won it, we wouldn't have had the belief afterwards to go on and win the All-Ireland the following year. To go four years without winning a championship game and then to win an All-Ireland? I don't think it would have been realistic.

The obvious game that I should talk about is the 2013 All-Ireland final. In relation to magnitude, it was the biggest game that I played in. But in relation to significance, the game that was biggest for me was the 2012 All-Ireland Qualifier against Dublin.

It was knockout championship at that stage. We had lost to Waterford in the first round of the Munster Championship. We were gone if we'd lost to Dublin.

Dublin were a serious team at the time. In 2011 they won the league and got to the All-Ireland semi-final. Then in 2013 they won the Leinster Championship and were probably within a sending off of getting to the All-Ireland final. Dublin were an excellent team under the great Anthony Daly.

I had been on the panel since 2007. We had gone three years... 2009, '10 and '11, without winning a championship game. Then we lost to Waterford and so the Dublin game was huge. For me, as a hurler growing up, before I looked at Thurles or Croke Park, Cusack Park was always the place I wanted to play. It was always the place I even wanted to train in.

As a Clare hurling man, there's no better place to be than Cusack Park on a Saturday evening when the sun is splitting the rocks in front of a full-house. I'd been fortunate enough to experience it on a few occasions, including in 2007 against Galway. Again, that was also a Saturday evening and the sun was out.

This particular one was just an unbelievable evening. The place was absolutely packed to capacity and the buzz of just running out in front of the Clare crowd was mind-blowing.

Cusack Park is our stadium, our house.

When it's full and you have the Clare crowd behind you, there's nothing that compares to it. For me, it's better than Thurles or Croke Park. It's just a phenomenal place.

As for the game itself, it wasn't an epic by any means. It was a cagey enough first-half and at half-time we were 0-11 to 0-7 down. While I was okay, I wouldn't have been standing out.

Then, a minute into the second-half, we were down to 14 men. Dublin kicked on and got two points after that. They had moved it out to a six-point gap... 0-13 to 0-7.

At that moment, a man down and *down* six points, against one of the best teams in Ireland, we could have gone on and got absolutely hammered.

We found something. I don't know what it was!

We clawed it back, point by point. With the Clare crowd behind us, every single score we got would put the hair standing on the back of your neck. Eventually, Darach Honan manufactured a 21-yard free and Tony Kelly, on his debut, stepped up and stuck it.

After that goal, we kept a two or three-point lead and ended up beating Dublin by three points.

I didn't play particularly well in the first-half but at some stage in the second-half, something clicked. I know it's a cliché when people say... 'Play with the shackles off!' but that's what we did.

Sometimes in games, especially as a defender, you go for a ball with a bit of caution. But for whatever reason, when we went down to 14 men, we said we can go out here and get hammered or else just absolutely go for everything.

I've watched the game back a couple of times and everyone on the field just went for every ball with pure abandon. We attacked everything. There was no caution.

Everyone said we might as well have a go here.

I had been going to National League games in Ennis with my brother since I was seven or eight. To be out on the field with the Clare people supporting you like that was unforgettable. Cusack Park is closed in, more so than the likes of Thurles or Croke Park. I'd compare it to the old Thomond Park atmosphere when it was full.

It was a huge step for us and for me personally. If we'd gone another year without winning a championship game, that would have been four years. Serious doubts would have been coming into your head… wondering were we at this level at all?

We got a huge amount of confidence as a group from it. When we were going back into training that winter, there was an extra little pep in the step from everybody, I felt. I'm not sure would that have been there if we'd gone four years in-a-row without winning a championship game. It was a big step and it gave us the confidence to go and achieve what we eventually did.

I often feel sorry for the players in the 2020 and '21 championships, not being able to play in front of capacity crowds or any crowd at all in '20. It's a massive driving factor. I experienced something very similar in 2007 when we played Galway in Ennis.

Outside of the game, it was the occasion; Daly was bringing Dublin to town.

The streets were packed from really early in the day. There was a feel-good atmosphere around the town. There was something very similar in 2007 when Loughnane brought Galway to the park. They were two very similar games.

Even the scorelines were similar enough. They were two of the greatest days I've ever had in a Clare jersey. You're in your own house and the house was electric.

Dalo's name wasn't mentioned once.

I put that down to the respect that we had for Dalo.

But we did get a kick earlier in the week. The draw was made on the Monday morning and one of the Dublin players tweeted… 'Perfect draw'. That's all we needed.

The following night in training, we had a group chat among the players. I spoke about it and said if that didn't make our blood boil, I didn't know what would. We thought it was a little bit of arrogance on their behalf, that they were looking down on us.

Fair enough, they were ahead of us in the rankings but as Michael Jordan would say… We took it personally. Small little things like that can make a big impact.

We played Limerick the following week. We put up a good performance but we lost. It was our fourth time playing them that year and we had beaten them three times. But even though we lost to Limerick, the fact that we had beaten a big team in Dublin was huge for us.

We were beaten by Limerick and it mattered, of course, but for that group at that time, we had beaten a good team in front of our home crowd. That was the bit of motivation we needed going into the winter.

In Whitegate, we haven't been blessed as a club to have players regularly on county panels down through the years. You could nearly count on one hand how many we've had. But, at the time, when you're playing, you wouldn't be really thinking about that.

The support that I got from Whitegate, from the club and the people was massive. I remember when I finished up, the club had a dinner dance and they had a surprise presentation for me, which I was blown away by.

Naoise Jordan presented me with a framed jersey.

I didn't know anything about this. It was then you'd realise that there are a lot of people that really support you. To have one of your own on the big stage probably means a lot to a small club.

As for Clare, we had a young team; four lads who finished against Dublin were minor the year previous. We had a mixture of experience with an awful lot of youth.

We had put in a serious year's hard work. We had stepped it up that winter and spring.

On a personal note, 2013 was unbelievable. It started off with getting a call-up to the Railway Cup team. Munster won it and it meant an awful lot at the time. Then we went on to win the All-Ireland and, after that, Whitegate won the intermediate.

I was also kicking a bit of football with Cratloe.

I had an agreement with Colm Collins that when Whitegate were finished, I'd play with them. I went back with them and we won the Senior Championship. It was one of those years where every team I was involved with won.

In Clare, we're not blessed with winning All-Irelands regularly, and neither do we play in Croke Park often enough. I always feel that when we get up to Croke Park, we're a match for anybody. The problem is getting to Croke Park. After 2013, we had difficulty getting there and we couldn't kick on.

For us in Clare, winning anything is huge.

We're not one of the traditional counties. We're not a Kilkenny, Tipperary or a Cork. But ever since the boys kick-started things in 1995, we'd like to think we've done a bit.

Sometimes we're starved of success, but when we eventually do get it, it makes it all the sweeter. If we can win an All-Ireland every seven or eight years, I think the Clare public would be very happy.

PAT O'CONNOR

Tough experiences, like failing to start against Dublin in 2012, helped Pat O'Connor understand what needed to be done through the remainder of his career.

66

I'LL NEVER, EVER forget the disappointment. The first kick in the teeth in my career was when Fitzy told me that I wasn't starting against Dublin in the qualifiers in 2012.

I was crushed.

I suppose I hadn't anything to lean on, or the experience to realise that it would be okay. It was a different game back then as well. Subs were very much the subs, whereas now it's a 20-man game. I couldn't get my head around it, although in hindsight, I knew it was coming.

A few weeks before that, I was whipped off after about 45 minutes in the Munster Championship against Waterford.

Davy was well within his rights to take me off. I was quite clearly being targeted. The three Waterford lads I was marking that day were John Mullane, Eoin Kelly and Seamus Prendergast. Needless to say, I didn't stand up to it.

They were a seasoned Waterford team.

I don't ever recall anyone telling John Mullane or Eoin Kelly to go on me. They were doing it themselves. They could see that things were not going particularly well for me.

But you try to take tangible things, even out of games like this, that you can work on. I remember myself and Mullane were facing a sideline ball. Just before it was hit, he pushed me in the chest and ran off. There was an immediate separation of three or four yards.

He got the ball and put it over the bar.

That stuck with me ever since, to never let a lad do that again. You can learn a lot on a bad day. It's never a nice experience to look back on a performance that didn't go well for the team or individually for you as a player.

But I felt that I had to. Particularly at that age, you can pick up so much if you can sit through watching yourself perform badly and getting beaten in a Munster Championship match.

There was a long wait then for the qualifier game. It could have been five-to-seven weeks. There was no club action.

It was just training, training… training!

Management and players were unhappy.

We just wanted games. Then we drew Dublin in Cusack Park in the qualifier.

I had it in my head that I wouldn't go up into the stand; that I'd stay in the dug-out. That way, I'd be near Fitzy's eyeline if anything happened. Conor Cooney had been struggling with his groin or quad. Lo and behold, only about 10 minutes into the game, Conor got injured and he had to come off.

He was corner-back and, up to that stage, I had never played corner-back in my life. I'd have been closer to corner-forward.

Davy put in me in corner-back anyway.

What transpired was a special day with Dalo coming down with the Dubs. He had walked them down, through the town, from the Temple Gate Hotel.

We were a young team and we hadn't won a championship match in so long.

It was a very special day. I played okay, as well as a corner-back can. If you keep your man quiet, that's as much as you can hope to do.

Had I been given any insight into how to play corner-back? None. Absolutely zero.

I hadn't played there even in a training match. I think it was 2016 that I started playing in the full-back line again. There wasn't one word about how to play there but I didn't need it. I was so motivated that day that I wasn't going to be the weak link again.

It was a huge shot in the arm for me, to get back in and it really built up my confidence. It told me that I could compete at that level and just because you don't play particularly well on one day, all is not lost. If you're given an opportunity, you can work yourself back in again.

From a manager or a coach's point of view, it's slightly different for a defender. You don't want to be taking off your backs if you don't have to. You want your six backs to be settled.

Forwards might run out of gas. They generally say that you always want 12 or 13 places on a team to be nailed down… and the rest of them to be fighting for two or three places. They're generally the forwards because you want the backs to be settled.

Unfortunately, Conor Cooney's loss was my gain that day.

I believed then, that on the back of the run we went on with the under-21s and conversations I had with Paul Kinnerk, that they were going to give me every chance again to prove myself in 2013.

I've often thought about this; from 2009 to '11, I knew that I was making progress. I could feel improvements and I thought I was destined to nail down a place on the team.

I made my debut in 2011 with Sparrow (Ger O'Loughlin). Although the year was an absolute whitewash; typical young lad looking out for himself, I was listening to fellas telling me that I did okay.

We had shipped two desperate defeats in the championship, but without the benefit of experience, you'd have a few lads slapping you on the back, telling you that you had done well in your first year out.

Come 2012, I was playing Fitzgibbon and under-21 with my club, all around

February and March. Also Fitzy had told me that year that he was going to try me at centre-back on the senior team.

We were in Division 1B and we were tipping away okay. We played Limerick in the first game and we hockeyed them. Then we played the likes of Antrim and Laois and we were going away the finest. We beat Limerick again in the Division 1B league final and got promoted.

Then it came to that first championship match against Waterford. Everyone was telling us that we were going to beat Waterford and that we were going to have a crack at Munster. That didn't quite work out!

We went on to lose to Limerick after we beat Dublin. All of my good work seemed to be undone because I didn't play a minute against Limerick.

But I was able to fall back in with the under-21s. We knew that we had a really good team. We had Tony (Kelly) and Colm Galvin. They were coming in with three years to go. Myself and Conor McGrath were in our last year, so we had a nice balance.

A few years before that, in 2009, we played Limerick in the first round of the under-21 and I didn't even get a jersey. They also spelt my name wrong in the programme. I was down as Patrick O'Connell. I was thinking… How far away am I from making this team?

I don't know how they did it but that management group played games at every training session. The games were so intense. I've rarely been involved in a set-up since where that would happen. You could have a great game on a Sunday but it might dip on a Tuesday for whatever reason.

But with that under-21 team, every single training game we played seemed to be so intense. I was going okay in them… and Alan Dunne was in my ear, telling me to keep doing what I was doing.

I was brought on at half-time in the 2009 Munster final below in Waterford. They were after beating the Tipp team that had Paudie and Brendan Maher. It was my first bit of success with Clare. I'd had a typical Clare underage career up to that; fairly competitive but no medals.

I felt that I did okay that day and it was another step in the ladder. I was after coming off a very disappointing minor campaign.

I was brought on wing-back. I didn't expect to be brought on either.

I think I had been playing in the forwards in training matches. It was a good introduction to the more adult side of hurling, The hand-holding had stopped and you had to make your own way.

I was told about 30 seconds before the team came back out, that I was being put on. There was obviously a debate about who was going on. I met them coming out of the dressing-room and I was going in. It was definitely a case of learning on your feet but I think it stood to me.

You can build these things up in your head but it's just a game. Go out and play. The autopilot comes on and it's just a game. You're being picked for your attributes and you're not expected to do anything that you can't do.

After that game, the dressing-room was chaotic.

Pa Kelly from Clarecastle had a t-shirt that had one of John Minogue's (our manager's) favourite sayings. He had it sewn into the back of the t-shirt and he put it on in the dressing room as we were coming in off the field.

Before I had come into the panel that year, they had played Kilkenny in a challenge and John Minogue said, 'I want my defenders to be the three Ts today… tight, tough and ignorant!' John was caught somewhere between wanting to take the head off him or start roaring laughing.

We had the 10-year reunion a couple of years ago and Pa Kelly still had the t-shirt on.

The more I think about it, 2009 was madness. There were huge crowds going to matches and there was such a buzz around the place. The fact that the under-21 All-Ireland final was on in Croke Park added to it.

I remember that time as being a little bit crazy. Crazy is probably a word you'd use for the group as well. There were such diverse characters but they had such an influence on me. I was a young fella coming in and I know for a fact that half of them had never heard of me. But the welcome they gave me and (Conor) McGrath was huge.

There was great fun with those lads. They were a bit wilder and, thankfully, it was before smartphones.

I think they taught us something that we might have lost as the years went on, that enjoyment is a huge part of it… and having the craic.

In 2012, I remember going from the intensity of senior training… the analysing and all that goes with it, to the under-21, which was such a fun environment to be in. We were going out after games, and we won the Munster final in Ennis.

We beat Tipp and then went on to beat Kilkenny in the All-Ireland final. I was brought on as a sub when we won in 2009 and I thought we out-worked Kilkenny that day but we really out-hurled them in 2012.

Later that year, we went on to win the Senior B with Tubber. Hurling is the only show in town in Tubber. And maybe farming.

We don't have a massive pick in Tubber and if we lost anyone from one to 15, we'd really struggle.

One of the happiest nights I ever had was in 2013, being able to bring the Liam MacCarthy Cup into my local. You had men in their eighties; some of them have passed away since, and they had tears in their eyes.

I often think back to that Dublin game and then the under-21 campaign in 2012. After taking a knock-back, it convinced me that I could play at that level.

That year turned out to be the shot in the arm to drive me on for 2013.

You get knocks in life, but they don't have to floor you as long as you learn and get back up.

99

COLIN RYAN

CLARE 1-22 LIMERICK 0-18
All-Ireland SHC Semi-Final
Croke Park
AUGUST 18, 2013

The freedom Davy Fitzgerald afforded Colin Ryan by playing him further out the field made a world of difference (above, Colin celebrates the All-Ireland victory in 2013).

★ **CLARE:** P Kelly; D O'Donovan, C Dillon, D McInerney; P O'Connor (0-1), Conor Ryan, B Bugler; T Kelly (0-4), C Galvin (0-1); J Conlon, P Collins (0-3), **Colin Ryan (0-11)**; C McGrath, D Honan (1-0), P Donnellan (0-1). Subs: F Lynch for Conlon, C McInerney (0-1) for Honan, N O'Connell for Galvin, S O'Donnell for McGrath.

★ **LIMERICK:** N Quaid; S Walsh, R McCarthy, T Condon; P O'Brien, W McNamara, G O'Mahony (0-2); P Browne (0-2), D O'Grady; D Breen (0-1), J Ryan (0-1), S Hickey; G Mulcahy (0-1), D Hannon (0-2), S Tobin. Subs: C Allis (0-1) for Hickey, S Dowling (0-6) for Tobin, N Moran for Hannon, T Ryan (0-1) for Allis, K Downes (0-1) for Breen.

THE ACTION

CLARE HEADED FOR Dublin neither fearing Limerick nor the occasion. Their opponents had been crowned Munster champions that summer and there was an air of confidence amongst the Limerick supporters that an All-Ireland final appearance was there for them.

Perhaps the weight of that expectation held back Limerick on the field. They looked tense and uncertain in their play, while Clare zipped around without a care in the world, with a glut of young players, who had played in the 2010 All-Ireland minor final and the 2009 under-21 final, both in Croke Park.

Clare deployed their captain Patrick Donnellan in a sweeping role and it worked to perfection. His team were on fire all over the field. Defensively, Clare limited the starting Limerick forwards to three points from play, while Declan Hannon had a difficult afternoon on free-taking duties. He was replaced in that role by Shane Dowling, but Limerick's jitters had spread throughout their team.

Colin Ryan excelled in his free-taking and in general play, while Darach Honan's 12th minute goal ensured that Clare kept Limerick at a comfortable distance all through the game.

With Clare deploying a sweeper, Tom Condon was Limerick's spare man. However, the five Clare forwards worked diligently when not on the ball and that curtailed Limerick from putting together any notable phases of play.

Tony Kelly and Colm Galvin, so impressive as underage midfielders, teamed up in the middle of the field in Croke Park for the seniors and hit a combined five points from play.

Clare looked very assured as they booked their place in the 2013 All-Ireland final, their team an average age of 23. It looked as if the years ahead would regularly feature Clare at the business end of the championship.

It certainly did in 2013, when they met Cork twice in the All-Ireland final, avenging their earlier defeat to the Jimmy Barry Murphy-managed team in the Munster Championship.

★★★★★

66

PADDY DONNELLAN TOOK off up the field, from his sweeper's position, about five minutes into the game. I saw him and hit him with a cross-field free.

It wasn't planned, and it wasn't practised.

It was probably one of the best balls I hit. I don't think he even had to break his stride. From the start, it just felt like we were on it that day.

That 2013 All-Ireland semi-final against Limerick is one of two stand-out games for me. The other is the 2012 county final when we (Newmarket-on-Fergus) beat Cratloe.

Before the Limerick game, there was an air of confidence. It wasn't cockiness, but everybody was really confident that we had a right good chance of winning. The warm-up was flawless. There are days when you're thinking you need to get your second wind, or you need the game to start as quickly as possible... but that day it was just so calm.

Even at half-time, there was no roaring and shouting and there was plenty of roaring at times with Davy. Everybody was just very calm throughout the whole day. It was a surreal experience; that's why I remember the game so fondly and so accurately.

There was no sense of panic. It was such a controlled day and when we won it, I felt unbelievable... having started out in 2007 and for six or seven years prior to 2013, we were absolutely crap.

There were 70,000 people at that game, which was the biggest crowd any of us had played in front of; our first time playing a massive senior game in Croke Park.

I teach in Limerick and to have the game I had that day vindicated a lot of what I had gone through in the early part of my career. So many people say that they never got to play in an All-Ireland final; and to think that we were going to be in an All-Ireland final after... it was crazy.

Limerick had beaten Cork in the Munster final that year. The sun was shining and I was there that day with my dad. We struggled to get out of there, such was the euphoria.

I wouldn't have had a particularly hard time against Limerick underage. We weren't that successful either but we gave them an awful hammering in Cusack Park in 2009 on our way to the under-21 All-Ireland. Their younger lads, like Declan Hannon and Shane Dowling, were only coming through at that stage. They were a bit younger and we probably felt that we had that bit more experience.

Declan Hannon had a horrible day on the frees and, I suppose, the big story afterwards was the difference in the free-takers. While that wasn't the only reason we won that day, it definitely helped. Every time we were putting over a free and they were missing them, it was a nail in their coffin and I think it sucked the confidence out of them.

I remember texting Declan about two days later. I had been *there*. He was quite young at the time but he's gone on and had his success, so I don't feel too sorry for him anymore.

That year, I had become a bigger cog on the team. While I had been talked about for many years, consistency and contributing to the team was my problem. I felt that when I was put further out the field under Davy, I was able to contribute a lot better. I felt that was my game and coming off the confidence of winning my first county championship with Newmarket in 2012, and playing that role, helped me to feel I was at the pitch of the game.

I definitely enjoyed that rather than being in corner-forward. That's one of the hardest positions to play in. Sometimes you're living off scraps and you could get one ball every 15 minutes. When I got on that roll in 2013 of contributing more, I felt more important.

Going into the Limerick game, I felt that everything clicked.

I had played well against Galway in the quarter-final and I had a good run against Wexford. I actually came off in that game and Davy said it was to give me a rest for five minutes, but I was brought on for extra-time straight away.

You kind of felt important and Davy instilled that in me.

Do I agree with everything Davy does? No but I'd have no All-Ireland without him. When all the lads involved talk about it, we know that he definitely changed the scene.

I just felt so free that day against Limerick. I think if we had tried anything, it would have worked. I still feel it to this day; the last 20 minutes were so enjoyable because we were so in control. We were thinking... *Let's enjoy this...* because we didn't get too many days in Croke Park where we were able to soak it in a small bit.

There's nearly always stress.

There are very few games you play in where you can take it in. A five or six-point lead in hurling is precarious. But that day the boys in the full-back line were in so much control. The ball was going into them and coming back out again, fast.

Limerick had pushed so high up the field that they nearly had created a clog-up at their end of the field. The space at our end was just phenomenal. I distinctly remember getting a ball and having about 50 yards of space to run into. I was asking myself... *Is this real?*

A lot of things came together and it was probably our most complete performance. The Limerick supporters were so flat and the Clare crowd were loving it.

It was our first big day out since the 2005 All-Ireland semi-final against Cork.

The Clare supporters were crying out for a team to come along and get behind. I think the Clare crowd really enjoyed that day. I know my parents certainly did. They don't get too many stress-free games, especially with me being a free-taker. But *they* even enjoyed it that day.

In my early days with Clare, especially when I was playing corner-forward, I always felt that if the ball wasn't coming in, you're nearly looking over your shoulder. Then you go out to hit a difficult free but you're not in the game.

If you miss the free, you're looking over your shoulder even more.

From 2011 on, I had started to separate the two. I really had to look at my overall game. There were plenty of days when I hadn't scored from play, but I was contributing. The work I was doing with Paul Kinnerk from 2012 on, it was a case of... *This is a free-scoring opportunity and there aren't too many lads who want to step up.*

To anyone who underestimates free-taking, I often say that somebody has to do it and each one counts the same as a point you get from 90 yards. I was able to separate it as time went on and when I look back, there were times when things weren't going one hundred percent right for me in general play, but frees were something that I could control.

Some of the lads that I have great regard for are lads that wouldn't necessarily get the plaudits from 2013. The likes of Domhnall O'Donovan, Cian Dillon, Pat O'Connor and Conor Ryan, for instance, didn't get the plaudits that Tony Kelly and Podge Collins got. But it takes a team to win and those lads did their jobs perfectly, without the bells and whistles.

We wouldn't have won it without the magic of Tony or Podge either. We probably got a pep in our step as well, knowing that Tipp and Kilkenny were gone. We had a sense that this was a real opportunity. People say we didn't beat Tipp or Kilkenny but there was nothing we could do about that. We knew we were one of the top four teams left in it and one of the four were going to win it.

There was a real sense of professionalism in 2013.

Everything was organised to a tee. Straight after that semi-final, plans were made for the final. They organised it so well; we had a great run-in and a great build-up to the final.

As for the 2012 county final, I can't remember too much about the build-up to it.

But if I could bottle up the 10 minutes after that game, I'd take it to my grave. The feeling that mam and dad and my aunts and uncles had; to have that feeling again is something that I'm still chasing.

We had lost enough finals and I tried to stay out of things, in the build-up, as much as possible. But at the same time with family ties and that, it was hard to stay out of it.

John Ryan had been the captain in 1981 and people were making connections between the two. I'd had a very good year for Newmarket that year and all that was in my head was to perform for the final.

Eoin O'Brien and James McInerney were man-marking Cathal McInerney and Conor McGrath. The two Cratloe boys were hurling unreal that year, but Eoin and James were unbelievable that day.

Seeing that happen, confidence grew throughout the whole team.

We had the rub of the green that day too.

Shane O'Brien Junior got two unbelievable goals off Sconey (Anthony Kilmartin) at full-forward. It was such a selfless performance and everything seemed to go right for us. We were ferocious until the very end that day and I think we wore Cratloe down.

Our history weighed on us an awful lot.

We had a good team from 2005. We lost to Clarecastle in the semi-final that year and we weren't far away from them. Out of all the finals we lost, the 2006 one is the one we look back on and think… *We had a real opportunity there!*

But maybe we just didn't have the experience to see it through.

Wolfe Tones had the likes of Frank (Lohan), Brian (Lohan) and BOC (Brian O'Connell). They were just that bit ahead of us. In 2008, we probably took it for granted with Clonlara. We probably felt this was our opportunity. They had just come up from intermediate. We didn't believe in 2006 but we didn't work hard enough in '08.

When 2012 came around, Bob Enright and the lads left no stone unturned.

Liam Sheedy coming in with us was a real coup. I remember Liam coming down the very first night. He'd have known a couple of us but on night one he knew every single player's name. He had asked Bob to send him a picture of every player.

He knew lads that were numbers 34 and 35 on the panel. He was calling them by their first names. If there was one moment where he got buy-in, that was it.

He drew everything out of every last player. Our matches in training were ferocious. We have struggled to replicate that but every club team does. The 'Bridge are probably the only club team in Clare that have the numbers to do that. We had a good intermediate team and when Liam came in, everybody was on board.

I think he just instilled that sense of belief and we worked extremely hard throughout that whole year.

There was barely a moment when we let up in any game. My only regret was the De La Salle game in Munster. Mikey McInerney had a chance of a goal and he absolutely riddled the crossbar. The ball ended up about 25 yards out the field. They went down the other end, got a goal and that was it. If it had gone over, we'd have been up a point and if it had gone in, we'd have been three points up.

There are plenty of people who go through their career without having either a county or All-Ireland medal. That 12 months in my career, I couldn't have written it. I think it's why I was able to step away from Clare in 2017 with no regrets.

People always ask do I miss it? Of course I miss Croke Park with 82,000 people. But what I don't miss is Caherlohan or Ballyline. What people don't realise is that for every game you play in Croke Park, there are 60 Ballylines or Caherlohans. My wife Louise was expecting and time was moving on. The balance wasn't right for me.

I remember thinking that for all the time I was spending away from home… *What am I really getting out of it?* And then you add in the meetings. They became two and a half hour meetings and you were gone, in total, for six hours.

Time was becoming really valuable to me and I don't regret it to this day. I could have easily been gone every night of the week and Louise probably wouldn't have given out to me but I don't regret it. But I suppose it was easier to go when I had had that success.

I always said this, and I said it to Bugs (Brendan Bugler) and Paddy (Donnellan) at the time, that when you get out, you won't go back in. When you get out of the bubble and realise that there are more things you can say 'yes' to than 'no', you won't go back.

Even saying yes to a stag party without having to check dates in the diary.

There are very few inter-county players who can step away and then go back into it. It was nine years full on. Every one of those nine years had tough times and great times, but they were all enjoyable.

The friends you make, you hold forever.

PATRICK DONNELLAN

CLARE 5-16 CORK 3-16
All-Ireland SHC Final Replay
Croke Park
SEPTEMBER 8, 2013

Patrick Donnellan lifts the Liam MacCarthy Cup in 2013, but he was left to wonder did the Clare team he led under-achieve?

★ **CLARE:** P Kelly; D O'Donovan, C Dillon, D McInerney; B Bugler, Conor Ryan, P O'Connor; P Donnellan, C Galvin; J Conlon (0-2), T Kelly (0-3), Colin Ryan (0-7); P Collins, S O'Donnell (3-3), C McGrath (1-1). Subs: C McInerney for Galvin, N O'Connell for Collins, D Honan (1-0) for O'Donnell, S Morey for Kelly. Blood sub: F Lynch for O'Donnell.

★ **CORK:** A Nash (1-0); C O'Sullivan, S O'Neill, B Murphy; C Joyce, S McDonnell, W Egan; D Kearney, L McLoughlin (0-1); S Harnedy (1-2), C McCarthy, P Cronin (0-1); L O'Farrell, P Horgan (0-9), C Lehane (0-2). Subs: S White for Egan, S Moylan (1-1) for O'Farrell, T Kenny for Kearney, C Naughton for McCarthy, K Murphy for McDonnell.

THE ACTION

THIS ALL-IRELAND FINAL went down as one of the most free-flowing and open in many years. Both teams simply went out to play hurling on the biggest day. Clare carried the greater threat, though, and in springing Éire Óg's Shane O'Donnell, they provided Cork with a conundrum that they could not find a solution to... O'Donnell lit up Croke Park with a stunning personal display, hitting 3-3 from play.

The 19-year-old was replaced a few minutes from time and when Darach Honan entered the fray, he too found the net. It was that kind of day for Clare, who were managed by Davy Fitzgerald, a two-time All-Ireland winner in the 90s.

Of course, Clare would not have had a second chance to win it had it not been for Domhnall O'Donovan's equalising point in the drawn game. Patrick Horgan had put Cork a point up and had they managed to keep an attacking line-ball in play, Cork would likely have won at the first attempt.

The replay featured 40 scores and eight goals, one of which was buried by Cork goalkeeper Anthony Nash, with 13 Clare players on the goal-line. Come half-time, Clare led 3-9 to 1-11 but Cork fought back and by the 53rd minute, it was level... Clare 3-10 Cork 1-16.

This time Shane O'Donnell came up with a badly-needed point and this was followed by like scores from John Conlon and Colin Ryan.

Cork hit back with a Seamus Harnedy goal but then Cratloe's Conor McGrath raced away from the men in red and put away his side's crucial fourth goal. Clare added three points, before Cork goaled again; this time it was Stephen Moylan.

Honan's goal sealed it for Clare, securing an epic fourth All-Ireland crown and their first since 1997.

★★★★★

❝

WHATEVER IT WAS, I had a feeling that we were going to perform. You get a great comfort from that feeling. It doesn't happen every day.

There would have been days going to games and you kind of knew that the preparation hadn't gone well, or you were missing a few lads with injury. For the 2013 final and replay, I had a feeling that we had a great chance.

The youth in our team had great energy but, at the same time, they were performing really well. They were the main players on the team and that gave us all a lift. It allowed us to play with a bit of freedom and abandon. It suited our style.

For most of my time, I was losing with Clare. Not even winning a game, let alone thinking that you could go on to play in a Munster or All-Ireland final... or win it. It was a complete change.

In 2012 and '13, the whole group had a different mindset.

That came with the professional approach and with the additional players. It came with having more of a focus on tactics and conditioning.

We had awful low days, like up in Salthill getting a hiding from Galway in 2011. But it's cyclical. You can be the worst in the world today and the next thing, on top of the world. That's high-level sport.

In the drawn All-Ireland final, Cork had a line-ball, when they were a point up. Stephen Moylan took it and put it wide. If he had kept it in play, the game was over. When Patrick Horgan put them a point up, that was the only time that Cork were ahead in that game.

The reality is that we could have blown it.

You see it in all the high-level sports. The margins are so, so small. There's a huge amount of nuances that have to go well and that's why you appreciate teams that are incredibly consistent. Teams like Manchester United in the 90s, the Kilkenny hurlers and Leinster Rugby. It's not easy to replicate it or to create a culture and seamlessly bring players in and out. You can get a bit of luck or be at the other end of the stick, as Cork were that day.

There were a good few years, in the middle, when we just weren't at the races. We probably didn't have the quality of player or the consistency. They started coming in then in 2011, '12 and '13 from the under-21s, after all the good work that was done at underage by Paul Kinnerk, Donal Moloney and Gerry O'Connor.

When the talent comes through, you have to foster it, bring it together and ultimately try to deliver. When you get a chance, try to make sure that you take it because there's no guarantee that you'll get a second chance. We got a chance in 2013 and, thankfully, we took it.

Fitzy had come in at the start of 2012 and had shaken things up. There was a natural lift, although we weren't performing great in 2012. We made a few strides but we didn't get to any significant heights. But you could see there was a progression from the start.

It was a real privilege and an honour for me to captain Clare. It's something that I hold dear and I'll always love the fact that I was chosen as captain. Davy approached me in 2012 and asked how would I feel about it? I said, 'No problem!'

I felt that I could bring something to it and help along the lads.

There was probably a handful of us who were senior members of the panel at the time. One of us was going to get the captaincy because there was a big gap then to the next generation. They were very new to the panel and it probably would have been added pressure for someone like that.

Over the years, you forget how things happened but coming up to the Galway game in 2013, there was a feeling that we were an excellent hurling team, but maybe we were not dogged enough at the back. That's how I ended up playing as a sweeper.

I think it came with the fact that we had so many young lads in the team. We wouldn't have been overpowered but, at the same time, we didn't have a standard full-back and centre-back pairing. We were trying to make positions fit. In the backs, we had six lads who could play in any position and I think that meant that we played a bit loose.

The thinking at the time was that it might be no harm, for the Galway game, to have an extra bit of cover and to see how it went. Galway had an excellent forward line with serious speed and Joe Canning was playing on the edge of the square. We were trying to nullify those threats but there really wasn't a huge amount of discussion about it. It just happened. We did it for that game, for the Limerick game and we chopped and changed a bit for the final and the replay against Cork.

I think more was made of it by everybody else than by us.

It wasn't something that we practised a whole lot. We did for a couple of weeks before the Galway game and in the run-up to the All-Ireland, but it was never the main focus or talking point.

What it has developed into with other teams is much more structured and an actual tactic. Back then, it was something we felt we might need to use and if we didn't need it, we just got rid of it.

Teams were kind of unsure how to deal with a sweeper, as opposed to it being an extremely effective tactic. I think it just made players unsure of their own role. It wasn't a new tactic, when we did it, but it was new for that era.

I think that teams didn't know how to approach it.

We saw that within a year or two, teams got a handle on it. Whether they pushed the centre-forward up on top of the sweeper or man-marked the sweeper, they found ways of doing it. It slipped under the radar that year and it gave us a little bit of an edge on the day if we needed it.

If we didn't, we weren't too reliant on it.

We had a bad game against Cork in the Munster Championship in 2013, but it felt like there was a good group there and a mix of youth and experience. There was a different mindset from Fitzy and a new vigour towards achieving and getting the best out of ourselves. We definitely didn't think that we were going to win the All-Ireland that year but there was a feeling that we were improving and could maybe make strides in Munster and start getting more consistent.

We were a team that probably wasn't considered as in with a chance of getting to an All-Ireland final and, when we got there, I didn't feel that there was much pressure on us. But for the semi-final against Limerick, we both felt that we had an equal chance of getting to the final.

There was a bit more of a focus for that game. The fact that you're moving to Croke Park; there was a natural step up, with everything that comes with it. There was probably more pressure and a glare on us for the semi-final, and what happened afterwards probably just rolled along.

We always went by train. We flew up when I joined the panel, under Dalo, in 2006 but they stopped doing that. In 2013, we went up by train to St Pat's in Drumcondra.

We had a puckaround and a stretch there, and went into Croke Park from there. The train was nice, in that you could mix a bit more. We used to go up and down on the bus, but we loved the train. It was a good routine and it definitely worked for us.

I find myself trying to remember what things happened in what game, apart from the pivotal things like Dunny's point or Anthony Nash's shots on goal the second day. You remember all those things but a lot of other things roll into each other.

We had excellent forwards and that was what really gave us the platform. The six lads were dangerous. Someone different would always take the limelight. Conor McGrath was brilliant and then Podge was excellent.

The focus was constantly switching from player to player. It wasn't as if it was on one main player and he'd be the best guy every day and would get 1-12 or 2-12. Everything was being spread around pretty well, which is what you want. The backs then don't have just one person to focus on. It really worked.

Everyone that came on had an impact.

When we won and I was going up to collect the Liam MacCarthy Cup, I was definitely aware of its significance. I got flashbacks of Dalo going up the steps of the Hogan Stand in 1995 and '97. I was brought up watching the Clare team of the 90s.

When I came onto the panel, I was lucky in that Lohan, Lynch, Seánie Mc and Fitzy were still playing. I got a brilliant insight into what it took to win; the drive and mental strength they had. The feeling of pride and respect they had representing Clare and giving it their all.

They helped me along when I was younger and all of those things came into my head when I became captain and got to lead out the team. You're not thinking about it a whole pile but you're conscious of it, and you feel that tradition coming with you.

Why didn't we follow up on 2013? Loads of us would have met up since and talked about it. We honestly don't know why we didn't drive on. At the time, we thought we were doing what we should have been doing.

In hindsight, did we take the focus off ourselves? When you listen to the likes of Jim Gavin or Joe Schmidt, directors of sport if you like who can give an overview, we might have taken our eye off the ball.

We weren't the finished article in 2013.

We still had a huge amount of things to work on and we probably should have brought the focus in on ourselves a bit. Maybe we should have added a couple of players and kept the focus on our own standards. I don't know, to be honest, because at the time we thought we were doing all of those things.

There definitely is a feeling there that we didn't get the best out of ourselves. When we won as a young team - although I wasn't young - maybe we didn't have the strength of mind to work on the things we needed to work on; make ourselves hard to beat and be consistent.

We've gone through loads of things on loads of nights, trying to work out if there was one thing we shouldn't have done or something we didn't do enough of. It just goes and before you know it, you've lost that bit of momentum.

You've lost that feeling that you're kind of unbeatable. That's hard to get back when you're struggling in first and second round games. But, thankfully, the team nowadays are a lot more consistent and hopefully we'll see someone else up on the steps of the Hogan Stand very soon.

My club O'Callaghan's Mills is a small club, like most others, with a great history in the GAA. It was an unbelievable honour for me to represent my club on that stage along with Conor 'Rocky' Cooney.

After we won the All-Ireland, we brought the cup back.

There was a parade and a presentation in the village. It was unreal. Myself and Rocky would have grown up watching the teams of the 90s and to do it in our own village was my boyhood dream. I can have no qualms or complaints about my career.

I'll always cherish that time and those moments.

I'll never over-achieve like I did that day for the rest of my life. I'll forever have it with me and I'm just extremely proud to do so.

CONOR RYAN

CRATLOE 0-14 CRUSHEEN 0-6
Clare SHC Final
Cusack Park
OCTOBER 5, 2014

Conor Ryan (left) celebrates with Cathal McInerney and David Collins after Cratloe defeated Crusheen in the 2014 Clare county final.

★ **CRATLOE:** G Ryan; S O'Leary, M Hawes, D Ryan; S Chaplin, **C Ryan**, E Boyce; M Murphy, L Markham (0-1); S Gleeson, P Collins (0-1), S Collins (0-2); C McInerney (0-2), G Considine (0-1), C McGrath (0-6). Subs: D Collins (0-1) for Gleeson, B Duggan for O'Leary, D Browne for Considine, J O'Gorman for D Ryan, P Gleeson for Chaplin.

★ **CRUSHEEN:** D Tuohy; J Greene, Cathal Dillon, A Brigdale; C O'Doherty, Cian Dillon, S Dillon; P Vaughan (0-5), F Kennedy; G O'Donnell, J Meaney, A Tuohy; C O'Donnell, G O'Grady, C Vaughan (0-1). Subs: D O'Doherty for A Tuohy, J Fitzgibbon for Meaney, Cronan Dillon for G O'Donnell, C O'Loughlin for Brigdale.

THE ACTION

THIS GAME WILL not be remembered for the quality of hurling but it was the first step in Cratloe's aim of securing a senior championship double for the boys in blue.

The following week Cratloe won the Clare Senior Football Championship for the first time, also completing the double in Clare for the first time since 1914.

To make their achievement even more remarkable, Cratloe featured 12 dual players. Many of those players had won senior All-Ireland medals with Clare in 2013 and played pivotal roles in Clare's three in-a-row All-Ireland under-21 successes. This achievement was closer to home though and once Cratloe got a scent of a double, there was no stopping them.

This was a turgid encounter but Cratloe did their business in the first-half and led 0-9 to 0-2 at the interval.

Gearóid Considine, Conor McGrath with three points, Seán Collins, Liam Markham and Cathal McInerney put over first-half scores for Cratloe, which combined to put them in a commanding position. Crusheen only managed three points from play in total.

Late in the second-half, Cratloe hit four points on the spin from McInerney, Podge Collins, David Collins and McGrath to put them into a 0-14 to 0-4 lead. Crusheen put over the last two scores but the result was well wrapped up by that point.

★ ★ ★ ★ ★

"

WHEN I saw the happiness of the whole parish and of all my friends, I realised that I didn't really feel part of it.

That's why, the more I look back on it, I think of the 2009 county final as a defining moment in my life. It took me until 2014 to experience that feeling with Cratloe.

The reason I didn't feel part of it was because there was never even a chance of me coming on. I still prepared my gear the night before as if I might come on. I was wondering if I should bring two hurleys but if I had brought a baseball bat, it wouldn't have mattered.

I wasn't coming on.

A couple of days later, I said to myself that I wanted to be involved the following year. Really involved. In 2009, I had a lot of learning and growing up to do. I had been on the Clare minor panel and was no closer to making that team either.

The reason I didn't make it was because my attitude wasn't good enough. I'd be the first to admit that now. To this day, I still remember Donal Moloney bringing me into a shed in Scariff, when we were there training. The group was training and Donal and Gerry (O'Connor) asked me to do an extra bit in there with them. Instead of me thinking it was great because they were taking an interest in me, I was insulted and my attitude was deplorable.

It's a lesson I'll take with me forever from that shed in Scariff.

If someone takes an interest in you and is trying to teach you something, soak it up. Every day is a school day. You win or you learn.

You're only losing when you're blaming someone else. It was a great teaching moment from them, even if it took me a couple of years to be mature enough to realise what was going on. That was early 2009. They saw a bit of potential and I didn't value that.

Going on to 2010, things were going well and we were in a county semi-final against Clonlara. I had been playing the whole way but not particularly well. I got dropped and rightly so. I didn't warrant inclusion on the team but I remember how hard it hit me. The night I was dropped, I drove in the gate. I didn't want to go in home, so I just sat there and started crying.

The next thing, I saw Johnny O'Gorman pulling up in his car behind me.

Jesus Christ! I thought… *The hard man of Cratloe hurling is looking at me spluttering in my car.* I couldn't hide it. He saw me and he came up to the window and he let off a roar… 'GET OUT OF THAT CAR!'

He wrapped his arms around me… and if he didn't start crying himself!

I thought to myself… *This is a man who cares.*

He said that he realised then that it mattered to me so much. As luck would have it, the game against Clonlara was a draw. Between the drawn game and the replay, James Enright, who replaced me, broke his hand in training. So I got in by process of elimination.

We lost to Crusheen in the final. We got back to the county final in 2012 and lost to Newmarket. I thought… *Jesus, this is taking longer than I thought.* Things started getting better for me then. I started listening more. In 2009, I learned that I had two ears and one mouth, and that I had to start using them in that proportion.

So I started taking in knowledge and stopped spitting out what I thought was knowledge. Then 2014 came. It was the year after we won the All-Ireland with Clare. I had started to become more of a senior player on the Cratloe team, just by being on the county team. Lads on the county team are expected to help to get their club team over the line. You should relish that, and I did.

In 2014 with Clare, we lost to Wexford in a qualifier replay. We thought… *This isn't in the script.* We thought we were supposed to win the All-Ireland again that year.

Me and Seán Collins would always talk about hurling and football with Clare and Cratloe. We were sharing a house at the time. We got home that night and I said to him, 'Colly, if this is the year we're going to give a good go at the double… let's go at it!'

We went at it and momentum built. We had no injuries and lads were in great form. We started putting some really good hurling games together and we got back to the final against Crusheen. I was buzzing.

I just felt it was going to be our day.

I went into the old showers in Cusack Park, with the big, high ceiling and I pretended to be stretching. I was gathering my thoughts. I realised that I was back where I wanted to be, but I also realised that I was back as a fella that the team needed to step up today.

Barry Duggan came up and put his arms around me.

He just said, 'I know what this means to you today. I know you want to be on the field to win one'. I'm not an emotional guy but that nearly knocked the socks off me. I said to myself that in years to come, I didn't want to be crying in the team picture.

So I settled myself… we went out, we played and we won.

It was the least memorable game, I remember.

TG4 were probably reluctant to ever come back down to Clare to show a live game again. It was desperate. We won it 0-14 to 0-6. But it was an ideal game for a defender. I remember asking the ref what was left at one stage and he said, '10 minutes'.

Davy Ryan looked at me and he said, 'Jesus, all of this stopping and starting is great'.

The final whistle went. I hadn't thought about the 2010 incident in a while but the mind is a strange thing. I went straight for Johnny (O'Gorman). I said to Johnny that I'd never forget what he did for me in 2010.

'If you tell anyone I cried, I'll f**king kill you,' he told me..

But that's the thing with teams in Cratloe. I have never had a bad word to say about a fella I hurled with for Cratloe or Clare. The reason it felt so special with Cratloe was because they were your best friends and your heroes. Every one of my best friends, that I grew up with, were involved in that team.

I would not have left the house, when I was younger, without my hurley. Even if you knew you weren't going pucking the ball, you'd bring your hurley.

If one of the lads said, 'Do you want to call up for a game of soccer?'… you'd still bring the hurley. It was an extension of your arm. You'd walk down the road and if you saw Conor McGrath, Liam Markham or Barry Gleeson and if they didn't have their hurley with them, you'd be thinking there's something seriously wrong here.

I still think to this day that if I went up to Joe McGrath's house and if I didn't have my hurley in my hand, he'd send me home. You'd feel ashamed if

Jackie (O'Gorman) or one of the senior hurlers waved at you on the road and you weren't carrying your hurley.

You'd think that they would think all you were doing was playing at home on the PlayStation.

We grew up in a lovely parish but you realise what hurling means to people.

They're so honest. They'll give us stick when we deserve it but they want the world for us. To be able to repay them with a county title and to go on and do the double the week after was just incredible. For me, that game in 2014 was the culmination of five years' worth of thinking and thinking.

I never got the opportunity to play with my brother Diarmuid, something which is my greatest career disappointment. But he was water-boy that day, so at least we shared that.

2013 was my first year on the Clare senior panel.

I had been fortunate enough to be on the under-21 All-Ireland winning team the year before. It was full circle in my relationship with Donal and Gerry. They probably saw me coming into the under-21 panel and thought here is this young fella who doesn't listen and knows it all like he did in the shed in Scariff.

But I opened up to them and told them that I just wanted to play and that I'd do anything.

We played Limerick in February of 2012 in an under-21 challenge match. None of the Clare senior boys were there, so I knew I had a good chance of playing if I turned up.

They put me in centre-back and said, 'This is your jersey to lose!' So I thought... *Grand, I'm going to try and hold onto this.*

They showed faith in me when I hadn't given them much reason to three years previously. For that, I'll forever be indebted to them. We won an All-Ireland that year and the following year I was asked to join the senior panel. I wouldn't have played centre-back that much growing up but Jody O'Connor was our under-21 hurling manager that year. He decided to put me in centre-back against Clonlara. We lost the same game.

That was when we realised who Colm Galvin was. Donal and Gerry had been at that game and they decided to try me out there.

If you asked anyone, even my father or mother, when was my first championship game for the Clare seniors, they'd say, 'Oh, the Galway game'.

But I'd say, 'No. I came on for all of 60 seconds against Wexford the day Cathal McInerney got two goals in extra-time. All I remember thinking was… *I hope there's lots of injury time here.* Wexford had a free and they put it over the bar.

I was running all over the place for the short puck-out but Pa Kelly rightly decided to hit it long. I worked up more of a sweat running onto the field, than I did when I was actually on. But I still have the jersey because, to me, it was my debut, even if no-one remembers it.

Before we played Galway in the quarter-final, Davy said that if we beat them, we'd win the All-Ireland. We were thinking… *Hold on a second, we're after struggling to beat Wexford.* But I owe a debt of gratitude to Davy. He showed faith in me, when not many would have seen it.

There was so much of the 2013 All-Ireland final that was outside of my control. Two or three days after the drawn game, Mike Deegan, our Cratloe manager, found a way to reframe it for me. He showed me a picture of me catching a ball that led to a score. Seamus Harnedy's hand was nearly catching my hand.

If Harnedy had caught that ball, instead of me and put it over the bar, which he did in another part of that game, and Cork had won by a point, there would have been no Man of the Match for Conor Ryan. So much of that game was outside of my control. Not many people would have thought that we needed me to have a good game for Clare to win.

I was a young fella on the team. I didn't control that, whereas in 2014 with Cratloe, I felt a bit more in control and confident in my ability.

I don't disregard playing for Clare in the slightest but growing up, I never thought I was good enough to play for Clare. My dream was to win county titles with Cratloe; hurling and football. Playing for Clare only became tangible in 2013, and very quickly. But for me, 2014 was the culmination of a long-serving goal. I look back and I smile when I think about it.

In 2016, I was diagnosed with an issue in my pituitary gland, which affects adrenalin and testosterone levels.

We played a Waterford Crystal game against Cork on January 25, 2017. The people who gave me my last Clare jersey were the men who had given me my first significant Clare jersey… Donal and Gerry. They called me in and said they might tog me.

Who's the last fella you'd like to be marking against Cork? They put me on Conor Lehane. There's a Sportsfile picture of me trying to run after him. I'm grimacing. I was with him for the first yard but it opened and opened.

Everyone knew that I wasn't coming out for the second-half. I had been stone useless. I should have been up front and honest. Donal said, 'Good man, we're giving you a break there for the second half'. I took 30 seconds to compose myself and went out to the sideline then.

I realised that week that the gig was up. It had gone full circle.

When I finished, I was lucky I had a good job to turn around to. I took a risk by leaving a very, very good job to go to Africa and figure things out there, while trying to give something back to a world that had given me so much.

I'm doing an MBA at Boston College at the moment and it must have been three months into my time over here that somebody found out that I had played hurling. It was just that I didn't want anyone judging me based on the past. If they were hanging around, I felt I must be doing something right.

I was here three weeks and the 2019 All-Ireland hurling final was on. I brought a few of my friends to watch it. I said nothing and we had a bit of craic. They couldn't get over the size of the crowds and how people in the pub were absolutely in awe of the sport.

They loved it.

How did they find out I played hurling? I had a lad over visiting from Parteen, Seán Quinn. He was visiting his girlfriend. So I brought them to a Boston College American Football game. At the time, the lads here didn't think that I had an athletic bone in my body. This particular day, we were throwing an American football around.

When it came to me, Seán said to them did they realise that Conor was fairly good at the hurling back home. I've good mates over here and thankfully they stuck around, not because I tried to play hurling.

GAA means the world to the people of Clare and Cratloe. There was this sense that this (retirement) was awful. I couldn't understand that. I remember saying to mum and dad that I had so much time back and there were so many things I could do with my life now.

It set off a chain of events. I wouldn't be in the U.S. without having left sport.

Was it tough to leave behind? It was but there's an opportunity in every challenge.

I didn't know what the future held and I still don't, but it's so much better than sitting feeling sorry for yourself. It's so much better to go out and explore life.

I'm very, very grateful for what I experienced on the hurling and football fields. I look back on it very fondly and without any regret whatsoever.

JOHN CONLON

CORK 2-24 CLARE 3-19
Munster SHC Final
Semple Stadium, Thurles
JULY 1, 2018

John Conlon in action against Galway in the 2018 All-Ireland Championship semi-final replay.

★ **CLARE:** D Tuohy; P O'Connor, D McInerney, J Browne; S Morey, C Cleary, J Shanahan; C Galvin (0-1), C Malone; P Duggan (1-7), T Kelly (0-1), D Reidy (1-2); P Collins (0-2), **J Conlon (0-5)**, S O'Donnell. Subs: J McCarthy for Malone, C McGrath (0-1) for O'Donnell, D Corry for Reidy, I Galvin (1-0) for Cleary.

★ **CORK:** A Nash; S O'Donoghue, D Cahalane, C Spillane; C Joyce, E Cadogan, M Coleman (0-2); D Fitzgibbon (0-2) B Cooper (0-1); L Meade (1-1), P Horgan (0-11), D Kearney (0-2); S Kingston, C Lehane (0-1), S Harnedy (1-4). Subs: R O'Flynn for Kingston, M Cahalane for Meade, L McLoughlin for Kearney.

THE ACTION

INSPIRED IN THE first-half, Clare couldn't sustain their efforts and their long wait for a Munster Championship, stretching back to 1998, went on after Cork beat them for the second successive year in the provincial final.

Led by John Conlon, who scored five first-half points, Clare looked very dangerous during the opening 35 minutes. First-half goals from David Reidy and Peter Duggan put them into a good position. Reidy's goal came after a Tony Kelly run, while Duggan's followed a long free from Donal Tuohy.

Much of their good early hurling was undermined close to half-time, when Luke Meade goaled and Mark Coleman pointed a lineball. Clare still led 2-11 to 1-10 at the interval but 10 minutes into the second-half, Cork had drawn level.

Clare gave everything they had but Cork had the edge and tagged on an array of points from Patrick Horgan and Seamus Harnedy. In the end, Cork were comfortable, although Ian Galvin struck for a late Clare goal.

Ever since Clare beat Cork in the 2013 All-Ireland final replay, the men from the south have had the edge. Clare's only championship win since then was a round-robin victory in Cusack Park in 2019.

As evidenced by the size of the Clare crowd that travelled to Thurles for the 2017 and '18 finals, there is a hunger in Clare to win a Munster title given that the barren streak stretches back more than 20 years.

Clare would have felt that 2018 was their best opportunity in many years but despite their best efforts, they could not get the better of Cork.

★★★★★

66

IT WAS ONE of those halves that I'll probably never experience again.

It's probably the best half of hurling I've ever played. Everything I touched went into my hand.

Every time I ran to a ball, it popped up and every little break was running for me. Throughout the round-robin, it was just one of those summers that kind of took off for me.

On the day before a match, I'd go down to the hurling field in Clonlara and Michelle, my fiancée, would hit a few balls into me. I'd pretend it was a Munster Championship match and I'd be working on movement and taking on the defender. Not at massive pace but I'd make sure I hit the shot.

In the first-half of that Munster final, I remember running back in towards the full-forward line and I was saying it was like I was in Clonlara with Michelle, hitting the ball over the bar. It was the weirdest feeling I had ever got.

It felt like the ball was being casually pucked into me and I was just hitting it over the bar, even though it was a Munster final in Thurles and the atmosphere electric.

Cork got a goal and a point just before half-time. *If we had gone in seven or eight points up?* It wasn't like we'd had a big lead but that 1-1 we conceded was a *big thing*. After doing all the hurling, we deserved to go in eight points up.

They came out after half-time and blew us out of it for five or 10 minutes.

We found it very hard to come back. It was disappointing because, as a team, that's the one medal that has eluded us. We had two chances in 2017 and '18 and we just didn't take them.

The second-half was the complete opposite for me. I only touched the ball two or three times and that was near the end, when I was brought out around the half-forward line. Maybe management could have brought me out the field earlier.

The two or three balls I won, just ran for me. I hadn't touched the ball in the first 15 minutes of the second-half. Maybe I could have been moved out earlier for 10 or 15 minutes and then go back in. But hindsight is easy. I have coached teams in my own club and it's very hard to make decisions on the line at times.

We just weren't getting ball in.

Cork had set up differently in the second-half. They had pulled back a bit deeper and we weren't winning enough ball around their half-back or half-forward line.

One of my biggest regrets is that we didn't win that match. I felt we were good enough. It was there for us.

The 2018 Munster round-robin championship brought a different vibe. You were playing week-in and week-out, and you were thinking about recovery the minute you'd finish a match. You'd focus on the first game but after that, the games ran into each other.

You either got on a roll or you didn't.

We played Cork in the first round and we had put a massive emphasis on them for five or six weeks. Donal Moloney and Gerry O'Connor were over us. Cork had been our bogey team for a few years. We went down to Páirc Uí Chaoimh and with 10 minutes to go, there was nothing in it. We thought we would drive out but we didn't and we were very disappointed after that. We had stayed in Cork the night before and, at the time, we thought it was a good idea.

Leading up to that game, I would have been detailed in my preparation but because we stayed the night in Cork, the hotel provided us with food. I usually have fish before a match but there must have been red onion in it, which doesn't agree with me.

In the match I felt gassy and my stomach was killing me. I got five points from play from centre-forward but I just felt really poorly going into that game.

On the Tuesday night before our next game, against Waterford, management pulled me aside at training and said they were going to try something different. They said they were going to put me in the full forward line and Peter (Duggan) in the half-forward line. I had played at full-forward with Clonlara but with Clare, I had never really played there, bar a championship game down in Wexford in 2014. I played well that day but I was generally seen as a No 10 that you could land a puck-out down on top of.

At the time, we didn't really have another option until Peter came through.

All week the tactics in training were built around Waterford's sweeper system and how we had to work the ball up the field.

Jack Browne got the first puck-out and he just leathered it down the field. I caught it and I think we won a free. I remember laughing at the time. Then Jack got the next puck-out and leathered it down the field again and we won a break off that.

Our whole tactical plan, going into that game, was to build the ball up the field and use support runners. But it all went out the window the minute that the route one option started to work. I remember Jack saying after the match, 'What's the point of going with all of these passes if we can get it to the edge of square and win it inside?"

Any time you have a championship match in Cusack Park is a magical experience. It's one of my favourite places to play. When it's full, it's a cauldron. Okay, if you're not doing well, they'll come down on top of you but if you're on top, they'll support you to the last.

Then we went down to Tipperary. We hadn't won in Thurles for 90 years. I thought we were poor in that game but we just managed to stay in it. I didn't think it was a great game and we weren't doing that well, until Podge (Collins) came on. He brought a bit of energy and got a point.

There was a period of time when I always said that if you made contact, you'd get away with throwing the ball. That was my ploy, so I threw it out to Podge and he laid it off to Ian Galvin and Ian stuck a great goal.

Limerick came into Ennis the week after.

In Ennis, we feel we can beat anyone. That Limerick team have gone on to win three All-Irelands but we'd never really fear them. In my time playing for Clare, we've had the upper-hand on Limerick. The place was electric and you couldn't get a ticket for love nor money.

We went out with an attitude that we wouldn't be beaten.

The cauldron of Cusack Park wouldn't have been what they would have been used to at the time. They learned a lot that day and I'd say it helped them a lot in the long run. I'd say that Paul Kinnerk and John Kiely sat down and made sure it never happened again.

It's a pity that we didn't get to the All-Ireland to see what would have happened in round two.

Every man died in his boots for Clare that day.

When we were in Thurles, Donal and Gerry used to bring us to Inch House. Because of what happened the first day, I wouldn't eat the food. I used to lie down for an hour in Inch House while the lads ate.

Gráinne Travers is our nutritionist, and I started making smoothies instead of eating the food whole. I haven't done it since but I got into that routine that year.

I'd blend the hake and veg into one. It was often left in my gear bag and the smell… Jack Browne used to look at me and say, 'How do you drink that?'

My theory was that whatever happened the first day against Cork, it would not happen to me again. I haven't done it since but it got a bit of traction at the time. The lads were calling me… 'Blender'.

The day of the 2018 Munster final, we got the bus in from Inch House and there were lines of traffic back past Borrisoleigh. I'll never forget that as long as I live. Everyone was getting out, waving their flags. It was a sea of Clare people and of colour.

Even talking about it now gives me shivers. It had that championship feel; playing Cork down in Thurles in the middle of summer.

When I got to 25 or 26, I started delving into mindset and working on the psychological side of it. But the main year I did it was that year. Cathal O'Reilly came in with us and he gave us a book. I read it and took out what I found was good for me.

I wouldn't be into visualisation. I'd find it very hard to sit down and say that this is going to be me running around, hitting the ball over the bar.

That wouldn't be me but I started using little things like self-talk.

I remember in the Limerick game I was doing well and at half-time they brought on Richie McCarthy. I had come up against Richie loads of times and he won the first two balls. I took two or three deep breaths and said… *Next ball* to myself. They were my cues.

I had watched the Richie McCaw documentary on his last year with the All Blacks. I took loads from that.

So I relaxed, took the deep breath and thought about what I could do better. I thought back to the two balls he won and changed my run for the next one. That worked and I started doing that for the rest of the second-half.

Before that, it would have got into my head when the Limerick supporters were singing, *Oh Richie McCarthy*. Then, all of a sudden, you're panicking going for a ball.

I really enjoyed the experience of working under Donal Moloney and Gerry O'Connor for three years. Personally, they helped me to become a better person on and off the field. They showed me what leadership is and how to apply myself better off the field.

They really put a big emphasis on education, life and what it means to play for Clare. I had never played under them, so my first time meeting them was in 2017.

I wouldn't say that their first year was my best but they put the challenge to me in 2018; I either was going to sink or stand-up. We built a great relationship with that management and I was disappointed to see them go.

After the Munster final, we got back on track and we played very well against Wexford in the All-Ireland quarter-final. Then we played Galway. We hadn't been in Croke Park since 2013. We love Croke Park; I feel it suits us.

We were really confident going into that game but we were terrible in the first-half. Galway blew us off the field.

Then management switched Colm Galvin to sweeper. He's a super reader of the game. At the time, Jamie Shanahan was wing-back and Colm was midfield. The minute either of them got the ball, I was moving. With other players, you wouldn't move until you saw them putting their head up. Colm and Jamie will see you moving and hit it, while they're moving themselves.

We came back after half-time and probably caught Galway off guard by playing a sweeper. I really thought when we got to extra-time, we were going to win it. Aaron Shanagher came on and got a great goal. I had a great chance of a goal; it hit John Hanbury's helmet, I think, as it was going towards goal.

We were two points up at the time.

Jason McCarthy came on to draw the game with a class point in extra-time.

In the second-half of extra-time, I ran out towards the sideline and slid on my left leg. I popped the ball off to Ian Galvin and he stuck it over the bar. I must have partially torn my PCL (Posterior Cruciate Ligament). I played on and it seemed fine.

It wasn't until after the match, I noticed that I couldn't get off the chair in the hotel afterwards. We got the train to Limerick and Michelle collected me. I struggled to get my foot into the car. I was all week trying to get right. I went down to Cork to meet Éanna Falvey. You're having one of the best summers of your life, playing the best hurling that you ever played…

I spent all week trying to recover.

I was never not going to play in the replay, but in hindsight I shouldn't have played. There was a chance that I could have fully torn it but I took the chance. On the Friday night, we'd always play a five or 10-minute game. I had to follow someone out around the middle of the field; I was biting my lip running after them.

I just didn't have the movement to get away from Daithí Burke. He's one of the best full-backs around. We'd had a titanic battle the week before.

In the first match, I used to slap him on the arse any time I scored a point to try and get into his head a bit. In the replay, I missed with my first shot and he went face-to-face with me. I remember thinking that it had come back to bite me on the arse.

I struggled through the whole game, movement-wise… and he's good in the air as well. It wasn't that I was going to dominate him in the air either. I just didn't have the same power and when you have an injury, you're always thinking about it.

With 10 minutes to go, they brought Aaron Shanagher on and I went out in the half-forward line. The problem at full-forward was that I needed to turn but in the half-forward line, I could run in straight lines and I was fine.

I won a ball or two when I went out and hit a point.

I'm the type that has to be pulled off the field, which is foolish. I got concussed against Cork in the Munster Championship first round in 2013. I played on for 10 or 15 minutes. I'm friends with Luke O'Farrell from Cork and he said that I asked William Egan twice, what way was I playing? I went over to Davy at one stage and also asked him… 'What way am I playing?'

After I came around, I thought that I had scored four points.

Joe O'Connor, who was our strength and conditioning coach at the time, told me two or three times that I had only played for 20 minutes. He said that I'd asked him so many times how had I played, that he told me I'd scored four points. I could hear the commentary in the ambulance on the way to the hospital and I thought I'd played well.

It was a privilege to win an All Star in 2018.

Colm Galvin has one from 2013 and Colm Honan was our other Clonlara All Star before that. We wouldn't be one of the traditional teams in the county but, as a club, we've made great strides. Our underage has gone from playing C and D to playing A and B. We've three fields, two sand-based and an astroturf.

When I was growing up, we had no-one on the Clare team.

The last county player we had was probably Colm's (Galvin) father Kevin. We had no-one involved in 1995 or '97. Ger O'Connell was on the minor team but he was playing with Broadford at the time. We had no-one really to look up to bar Ger and, I remember, Wayne Kennedy, who was from Parteen.

It was great to be able to bring some of that to the parish.

In 2009 we had six on the team that won the under-21 All-Ireland. We had nine or 10 playing inter-county at the same time between minor, under-21 and senior.

That was maybe our downfall with the club as well, that we had so many playing county. We always had about nine lads away with Clare teams, which made it very hard to organise us. When you get back, you only have a few weeks to try and get things right.

My family is heavily involved with the club. My father would have been over all of my underage teams. A lot of players came through and it was down to a few parents like my father, Eddie Horgan, Colm Honan and Seán O'Donovan. They brought us the whole way up.

I remember their elation after winning the 2008 Senior Championship. It came all of a sudden. We won the intermediate the year before and that was expected. Then we went on to win a Munster intermediate and the year after, we went on a run.

We got an easy group and we got out of it, although Crusheen hammered us. We played Kilmaley in the quarter-final and Colin Lynch was injured for them. We thought, that without him, we could beat them. We played Crusheen in the semi-final. We had the O'Donovans back from a J1. We won it well in the end.

We went into the final against Newmarket and there was nothing expected of us. When you're not expected to do something, the pressure is off. Things just happen and you go out with a free spirit.

After the final, someone said to my father that he wasn't getting onto the field and he said, 'Watch me!' He climbed the fence in Cusack Park and cut his hands.

He was bawling crying and hugging lads with his hands covered in blood. He went around and nearly hugged everyone there.

Then he came to me, looked, half-nodded and walked away. That was his reaction on the most satisfying day in our club's history!

When I was a young fella coming through, he'd be asking, 'Why did you miss that or why did you do that wrong?' Even though you might have played the best game you ever played!

We still cut the hurling field in Clonlara.

I always say to any teams or children that I'd talk to, to have gratitude and to thank their parents or coaches. Cutting a hurling field takes two or three hours out of your week.

That's why I try to help out as much as I can with the club in terms of fundraising and stuff. It's where we start and where we finish. We're trying to make it a better club for our own children in the future, nieces or nephews.

When we won the senior in 2008, we went to the county final the year after. We should have beaten Cratloe but they got the goal in the last minute to win it. From there on, we went on to compete in either the county semi-final or final, every year until the last two or three years. In my eyes, I was always very proud of it, although I know that we didn't get over the line since 2008. People would probably say that's an underachievement.

The 'Bridge beat us very well in 2015 and we have no excuses for that. We played Ballyea the year after and that was the one year that everything was done in terms of training and we had super management. We were five points up with about 10 minutes to go. Martin O'Leary got the goal and Tony Kelly came thundering into the game. He was after having a great battle with Oisín (O'Brien).

Even in the replay, we brought it back to a draw.

I got a ball and scored a point but it was waved wide. The night after, we were in Ballyea and Kevin Sheehan, who was in goals for Ballyea, told me that it went straight over the bar. It was a tight angle but the umpires thought it was outside. But he said it was well inside.

If we had gone a point up, that momentum would have been massive. They went on to play in an All-Ireland club final.

I've won an All-Ireland, a National League, and a Fitzgibbon Cup with NUIG. But if anyone asks me what's my best medal, it's the county championship in 2008. The All-Ireland was huge but the elation that winning a county championship gives to your family is unforgettable.

99

TONY KELLY

BALLYEA 4-18 THURLES SARSFIELDS 2-22
Munster SHC Semi-Final
Cusack Park
NOVEMBER 6, 2016

Tony Kelly celebrates with his father Donal (above, after beating Glen Rovers in the Munster final) during Ballyea's magnificent 2016 season.

★ **BALLYEA:** K Sheehan; J Neylon, J Browne, B Carigg; P Flanagan, G O'Connell, J Murphy; **T Kelly (1-10)**, S Lineen; N Deasy (0-5), P Connolly (0-1), C Doohan; M O'Leary, G Brennan (1-0), P Lillis (1-1). Subs: D Burke (1-1) for O'Leary, D Egan for Carigg, A Keane for Connolly, F Neylon for Egan.

★ **THURLES SARSFIELDS:** P McCormack; S Maher, S Lillis, R Dwan; D Maher, P Maher (1-0), R Maher (0-1); J Maher (0-1), S Cahill (0-1); B McCarthy, A McCormack (1-4), T Doyle (0-3); L Corbett, P Bourke (0-9), C Lanigan (0-2). Subs: M O'Brien (0-1) for Lanigan, K Dunne for Doyle, D Kennedy for Lillis, C Moloney for Corbett, L Corbett for Moloney, S Lillis for J Maher, C Lanigan for Dunne, J Maher for Lanigan, C Moloney for Kennedy, M Cahill for Corbett.

THE ACTION

AN EXTRAORDINARY WEEK for Ballyea culminated in even more thrilling fashion when the first-time Clare champions stormed beyond Thurles Sarsfields and into the 2016 Munster club final.

The previous Sunday, at the same venue, Ballyea had beaten Clonlara in a replay to get their hands on the Canon Hamilton Cup for the first time.

However, they left enough in the tank to tackle the Tipperary champions, who led by five points two minutes from the end of normal time. Ballyea looked finished but points from Tony Kelly and Pearse Lillis opened the door. Full-forward Gary Brennan fully opened that door a minute or so later when he cut through the Thurles defence and fired a superb equalising goal.

Nobody could believe it, least of all Ballyea. They sensed that they had a chance of reaching a provincial final, and extra-time scores from Kelly and Niall Deasy sent them on their way.

While Ballyea struggled for much of the second-half of normal time, they had made a great start, goaling twice inside the first seven minutes. Kelly put away a penalty, won by Deasy, while Lillis netted after picking up a break off Brennan. By half-time in normal time, Sarsfields had recovered and led 1-11 to 2-4. Ten minutes into the second half, the Tipperary men had extended their lead to seven points and they looked very likely to retain that lead.

Ballyea kept chipping away, and that last-minute goal from Brennan forced extra-time. Kelly put over three points in the first-half of extra time, while Damien Burke goaled, putting them into a 4-15 to 1-20 lead. This time it was Thurles who hit back, with Pádraic Maher goaling... it was game on again.

Niall Deasy nailed three late points, which closed it out for Ballyea.

★★★★★

❝

AT THE END of normal time, we were in the dressing-room laughing. We could not believe that we had come back and levelled it.

That Munster club semi-final against Thurles Sarsfields is probably the game I would think about the most, in terms of… *How did we win it?*

We'd won our first county championship seven days previously against Clonlara in a replay. You can imagine that lads weren't at home too often that week. We still had lads out on the Thursday. We trained in Gurteen on the Friday night before the Sunday because we had no lights in Ballyea.

Our coach Fergal Hegarty was running us up and down, and over and back the field, solely trying to sweat the liquor out of some lads, who were out around Limerick on the Tuesday, Wednesday and Thursday nights.

I remember starting the game on the Sunday and thinking that I had never played a club game at that pace. Thurles were playing at a *different* pace and level completely to what we were playing at.

I remember turning to Jack Browne at one stage and saying that it was like a county game. We were absolutely gasping for air and I don't know how things swung in our favour that day, but they did.

We got off to a good enough start. We got two goals, one from a penalty and Pierce Lillis got a goal. Then they took over and they were leading by seven points with six minutes to go.

We got a few points and slowly clawed it back to a goal.

There was about a minute left and we got a lineball on our own 21-yard line. Jack (Browne) hit a great ball to Gary (Brennan) and he won it over Paudie Maher. He went straight for goal and buried it. We took off then in extra-time.

I think they took off one or two lads that were flying it for them. We had so much momentum in extra-time, it was hard for them to claw it back.

In the week leading up to it, it wasn't so much about winning it. It was more going out to represent the county as best we could. We knew that we were coming up against a good team and reading the programme before the game, their team was littered with lads who had won the All-Ireland the year before with Tipp. It was only when we were in it that we sniffed that there was a chance there to win it, or to bring ourselves as close to winning it as we could.

The amount of work that the likes of Pierce, Stan (Lineen), Gary and Cathal Doohan did was unbelievable.

You have to have a blend. If you go out with 15 brilliant, skilful hurlers, who can hit off right and left and put the ball over the bar, it's a plus, but you need a few men around the field who are able to do the hard graft.

Those lads fit what we were doing, especially up front.

You see the likes of Cillian Brennan nowadays working so incredibly hard to get the ball to the likes of (Niall) Deasy, who can put it over the bar. It's selfless. Deasy will always put it over the bar but there's so much work that goes on before that, to get it to him and that's what those lads are absolutely excellent at.

We had experience of inter-county hurling ourselves in Paul Flanagan, Jack, Gudgy (O'Connell), and then Gary and Pierce from the football side of things. That was the springboard then to get to the All-Ireland club final in 2017. We felt that if we were able to beat Thurles Sarsfields, we believed that we were as good as anyone left.

I remember talking to Colin Ryan when I first joined the Clare panel. He always said that he never wanted to be the hurler that went back to his club and didn't really produce. Or that he was the county lad at his club but never really took the club game seriously.

That's one thing that stayed with me always, that when you go back to the club you always try to be at your best or somewhere near your best. I always try to perform my best every day I go out but you have that more at the back of your mind when you go out with your club.

You might have to do that extra bit.

In terms of the team that we've had since we were under-16 or minor, you're so used to playing together that you know your club lads better than you know the county lads.

My age group would have had Stan Lineen and Martin O'Leary, and Niall Deasy's age group had Pierce Lillis. They were always there from under-12 all the way up along. Under-10 was the only age group I didn't play with Martin, Stan or Damien Burke.

When we were growing up, the best team we ever had was the team that got to the county final in 2003. We looked up to them as if they had won six All-Ireland clubs in-a-row. We held them in such regard. When you grow up then and go one step further, win it and then win a Munster club and back it up with another county championship, it was really special.

I don't think that I would have played senior hurling for Clare only for the likes of Pierce, Stan, Martin, Joe Neylon or James Murphy. They allowed us to play A hurling against the likes of Sixmilebridge up along. Only for them, we'd probably have been down at B and C.

When I started out first, I played under-14 D aged nine or 10. I remember playing a game in Bodyke. That's the grade we were at. We had to go to Kilmihil and Cooraclare searching for the likes of Stan, Martin, Allyn Dalton and Damien Burke to try and give us something to get up and try to play B or A.

We were lucky enough when we got those lads; Fergie O'Loughlin came out and trained us. I don't think we've trained as hard since. We were training three and four nights a week at under-12 and then we'd have challenge matches at the weekend. We knew that the 'Bridge were doing the same thing below there. We met them in an under-12, 14, 16, minor and under-21 A final.

The only one we haven't met them in is a senior final.

We'd have grown up playing against lads like Seadna Morey, Jamie Shanahan, Alan Mulready, Kevin Lynch, Shane Golden and Noel Purcell. All of those lads are still there and so are the bulk of our lads.

If you asked an under-12 or under-14 team to train now like we did back then, you'd be pulled up on it. Parents would be going off the head. It was a different time and our parents were of the same make-up. Fergie was an unbelievable trainer and he brought our hurling to a different level completely.

The matches were almost easier than the training. Things started increasing in intensity between us and Sixmilebridge. We got the better of them in an under-12 and Féile final but they came back and beat us in an under-16 and minor final. I don't think I would have reached a good level, only for that training and those games at underage.

In 2016, it helped that we got a clear run at it. The county was out that bit earlier and we got to train a lot more together. The biggest thing was that training was so competitive. You're bringing the likes of Gary, Pierce, Gudgy, Jack and Paul out of an inter-county set-up where everything is so competitive that it's just natural when you come to the club field.

The club lads were unbelievable to train. When we came back, they upped their game even more.

One thing that keeps driving it is that we have a few club lads who wouldn't be afraid to call out a county player... or any player. That helps as well.

Everyone is on a level field.

It's probably more their team than it is our team. They're there all year round. We're swanning in around June, July or August and we're coming in for a six or eight-week block. They're slogging since the previous October or November, trying to keep the show on the road.

Before the Munster club final, I remember James Murphy coming to the pre-match meal and he was nearly asleep at the table, before we went out and played. He had cows calving and he said he'd normally go to bed at 9pm, get up at 12 midnight and do a shift until 2am. But that night he got up just before 12 and stayed up until the match the following day at 2.30pm.

He went out and hurled a stormer.

We have those kind of characters who add to the whole thing. They're tough men. Whatever they lack in hurling, they're worth anything when it comes to toughness, honesty and just hard work.

With Clare, a game that was hugely significant for us was the Limerick game in the 2013 All-Ireland semi-final. Going into Croke Park that day, it was just littered with green and white. I'd say we were out-numbered three or four-to-one.

In a way, it gives you an extra pep in your step. You think that we're going to send a lot of disappointed Limerick supporters down the road if we come out here and perform. If you have a massive crowd behind you, you can feel more pressure in other ways.

That day, with Limerick coming with so much expectation, we went out saying we were going to put an end to the party. They've got their time in the sun in the last few years, so I suppose it comes around in cycles.

It was a day when things didn't go well for them and everything seemed to flow for us. Every free went over the bar, and every pass or shot at goal seemed to work. There was a freeness in us. We went out saying that Limerick were Munster champions and they had it all to lose.

It brought through the confidence that we had coming from minor and under-21. We didn't really have much pressure on us but we thought that we were good enough to be there because we had won the last three under-21 All-Irelands. We went to Croke Park with no fear and, to a man, we hurled well that day.

The biggest thing I've learned, especially at inter-county level, is patience.

I don't mean patience in that you stand up and hope that the play will come down on top of you or down your wing. What I mean is, when the ball is in your area, you might have to make the same run maybe three times and not get frustrated that you don't get it the first or the second time.

I often found that if I made a particular run and I didn't get it, I mightn't make that run the next time. It's about learning that as long as it's the right run in the right place, keep doing it and eventually it'll come to you. If you look at the likes of Shane O'Donnell, he must make five or six runs before eventually he might get a decent ball that he can do something with.

That's the patience that you pick up the more you play.

You definitely know when you're playing very well.

It's hard to explain it. You mightn't be making every run possible but the ball just seems to be where you are the whole time. It's more effortless and off the cuff. You feel in that zone, where you know if you do get the ball, you're going to make something happen with it. Or if the ball drops in that vicinity, that you're going to get on it.

Other days, when you're not really involved in the play, you go searching for it that bit more. When you're in your late teens or early twenties, you can find yourself covering every blade of grass and then wondering why you were only on the ball three or four times?

When you're playing well, you look back and realise that you might have scored a good bit but that you weren't going back into your own half or didn't do much running. You can definitely sense when you're going well, versus when you're struggling and you go searching for ball.

You end up running yourself ragged for no reason.

If you play midfield, it's the one position where you can end up everywhere and anywhere. I've played most of my career in the half-forward line or midfield, but I definitely enjoyed going into the full-forward line in the last year or two. It's something different and usually you're on someone who is more used to being further out the field. You're bringing them into a zone that they're not used to playing in either.

In 2019, when we played Cork, Donal Moloney said that they were going to try me somewhere new. They put me into the full-forward line beside Shane (O'Donnell). He's so easy to play inside with; it didn't make the transition as hard. If you can play in a few positions, it's definitely a benefit.

Closer to home, I have to say that the club lads that allowed us to play A hurling, meant that we had a chance to go on and play for Clare. That's why when we play for the club, I try to do my best for them.

Going out and playing in Thurles in a Munster club final and in Croke Park was the reward for them. It was massive for all of us.

As good as winning with your county is, there is no better feeling than coming home to the one pub we have in the parish and celebrating there.

Printed in Great Britain
by Amazon

70415434R00139